GET OUT OF YOUR HEAD

A toolkit for living with and overcoming anxiety

By Brian Sachetta

D1397531

Dedicated to all those dealing with mental illness and the ones we've lost to it

TABLE OF CONTENTS

PART 1: ZOOMING IN

PART 2: ZOOMING OUT

DISCLAIMER

Many events and conversations within this book have been recreated from memory. To respect the anonymity of the people and organizations involved in those events and conversations, many names and details have been changed or omitted.

All attempts have been made to verify the information in this book. However, neither the author nor the publisher assumes any responsibility for errors, omissions, or contrary interpretations of the content within.

This book contains the opinions and ideas of its author. Its purpose is to provide helpful, general information on the subjects it addresses. This book is not meant to be used, nor should it be used, to diagnose or treat any medical condition.

For the diagnosis or treatment of any medical problem, consult your own physician. The author and publisher do not guarantee any specific results from reading this book or implementing the strategies described in it.

You, as the reader, are responsible for your own actions. The author and publisher specifically disclaim all responsibility for injury, damage, or loss that you may incur as a direct or indirect consequence of following any directions or suggestions given in this book.

PART 1: ZOOMING IN

INTRODUCTION

"Beta blockers? Tranquilizers? Are you freaking kidding me?!" I could barely get the words out of my mouth as I sat at my desk in disbelief of what I was reading. It was one of the first Sundays of my freshman year of college. I hadn't gotten much sleep. The night before was an unmitigated disaster – an experience that would likely go down as the most painful social interaction of my life.

I'd met a cute girl, Samantha, during the first days at school and was developing feelings for her. That previous night, she texted me. She was at a party. I was sober. She was coming over. I was nervous. Like *really freaking* nervous. I'd suffered my first panic attack with a different girl, Monica, just a few months prior and couldn't think of much else when it came to women.

I asked myself if I should down a few drinks, but wasn't sure they'd hit me in time. I went for a quick walk down the hall just to figure out what to do. I'd barely passed the study lounge when I heard her scream my name from the stairwell in front of me. "Briiiiiaaaaaaaan!" Holy crap. She said she'd be over in fifteen minutes. It had only been five and I wasn't ready. My heart pounded. I couldn't think straight. This was it, the very thing I feared most – another panic attack.

My mind raced as I fought the panic harder and harder. "Not this. Not now," I muttered as I fell into the chair behind me, hoping it would help me gather myself. Samantha sat down on the same chair, right next to me. "Oh no," I thought. "I'm toast." Within seconds of her sitting down, she felt my heart racing and screamed. "Holy shit, why are you shaking? Oh my god! What the fuck is wrong with you?!" My heart sank. She sprang up out of the chair in horror and bolted down the stairs nearby. I ran after her, beside myself that this was happening again.

She shot out of the stairwell and ran down the hallway to her room. I followed after her. As she punched in her door code, I pleaded with her, telling her I was shaking because I was so tired. She didn't buy it. She said she was feeling light-headed and just wanted to go to sleep. I didn't buy her story either. I watched her door close in front of me, then turned and headed back to my floor. It was, figuratively speaking, a very long walk. I went to bed that night dejected and frustrated. How would I prevent another panic attack from arising when I had no idea what caused them in the first place?

This question was at the forefront of my mind as I sat at my desk that next morning. I rifled through newly purchased eBooks on panic attacks and anxiety. I needed answers. This was college for crying out loud. It wasn't supposed to be like this. College was supposed to be fun, filled with crazy parties and tons of girls – not this struggle.

I spent hours that day reading as much information as I could get my hands on. The eBooks I purchased were rubbish, but they were the only published content I'd ever consumed on panic and anxiety. I gave them a chance. They advocated taking beta blockers, tranquilizers, and antidepressants. "Beta blockers?! I'm supposed to take beta blockers? What the hell is wrong with me?!" It was too much to take in. I felt like I was going to be sick.

GETTING INTO YOUR HEAD

Despite not enjoying the eBooks I purchased, one of them contained what was, at the time, an intriguing idea to me. The author explained that panic attacks arise out of situation-based anxiety,[1] the latter of which occurs when we identify an outcome we desire from a situation but don't know how we'll get it. In order to overcome this anxiety and avoid panic, he said, we need to see ourselves in the midst of

---

[1] Defined as the anxiety associated with specific moments in time or events such as a school dance or tryout.

these upcoming, scary events. For example, on stage, successfully performing a solo before a sold-out crowd.

I felt like I'd been using the strategy somewhat already, but hadn't mastered it. It made so much sense to me. I resolved to ramp up my efforts with it. The next time I felt nervous about an upcoming event, I declared, I'd picture myself fighting off my anxiety and achieving the results I'd set out to attain. Hopefully, it would work just like the author said.

Unfortunately, this strategy never bore the fruits I hoped for, despite the author's confidence in it. It took me years of banging my head against the wall to realize this. With more time and practice, I told myself, I'd master the strategy and make it part of my routine. But as the years went on, it dawned on me that, with this specific technique, there was no winning.

As it turns out, visualization, when it comes to anxiety, is a loser's game. This is because when our desires are intertwined with our fears, envisioning what we want also forces us to think about what we don't want. Sure, we want to successfully perform our solo, but we also want to avoid having a panic attack on stage. For many of us, thinking about the former begets dwelling on the latter.

Brooding on our greatest fears isn't something we always do consciously, and that's what makes this kind of visualization so hazardous. One minute we're envisioning our dreams, and the next, we're fighting our demons without even realizing it. The more we fight our fears, the more anxious we become and the less capable we feel of achieving our desired outcomes.

This is why I say visualization, in the face of anxiety, is so dangerous. It's a well-intentioned path, but an insidious one that often leads to ruin. I didn't know it at the time, but this very strategy was keeping me stuck inside my head, the place I needed to avoid if I were to evade my panic attacks and anxiety for good.

Unfortunately, so many of us approach life in this fashion. We overthink everything. We pre-plan every minute detail of our lives and hope there will be no unforeseen circumstances. We dive into our heads and attempt to reason ourselves out of anxiety much like we would a puzzle or logic game.

But life is no puzzle. It's not meant to be lived so analytically, nor is that required to achieve our desired ends in life. No amount of thinking or worrying about our fears will ever lead us away from them. The rabbit hole doesn't end, it just goes deeper the more we think. The only way back to the surface is to get out of our heads entirely.

THE PURPOSE OF THIS BOOK

The primary purpose of this book is simple: to show you what it means to get out of your head, and provide the tools necessary for achieving such a feat. To do that, I'll start by explaining what anxiety is and where it comes from. Then, I'll outline two sets of strategies for alleviating your anxiety – one that helps you lower your anxious reactions in acute, anxiety-provoking situations, and another that helps you get into fewer of those situations in the first place.

More than ten years have elapsed since that terrifying weekend in college. During that time, I've not only read just about everything I could get my hands on in regard to panic attacks and anxiety, but I've also gone through several key, anxiety-provoking situations that have forever altered my approach when it comes to mental health. Through these experiences, I've experimented with and developed countless strategies for dealing with my anxiety, and have found the ones that actually work for me. The purpose of this book, then, is to teach you those strategies in hopes that they'll work for you as well.

The secondary purpose of this book is to help those suffering from anxiety see their condition in a new light. Anxiety can be a difficult subject to talk about, let alone deal with. For many of us, it strips us of our confidence, energy, and faith. In this book, I'm going to show you how you can use your anxiety as a tool for reconnecting with yourself and what motivates you, then leverage that connection into an energy source for your greatest passions.

The purpose of this book is *not* to facilitate a discussion on psychiatric medication. There are two reasons for this. The first is I'm not a doctor and therefore not qualified to give advice on the subject. The second is my strategies are not centered around modern medicine. Though I've taken anti-anxiety medication in the past, I don't feel it's as effective *for me* as the strategies I'll present in this book.

Though medication is not a focus of this book, please remember it's only one of the many forms of treatment out there. Just like the strategies I'll present here, it may work *for you* and it may not. Only you and your doctor can make that determination. As you navigate your own journey, keep an open mind, evaluate what's helpful for you, and go from there. If you do decide to go the medication route, please just make sure you understand the potential side effects. As a rule of thumb, when in doubt, discuss with your doctor.

I firmly believe that anxiety is just an extension of our innate survival mechanisms. When we leverage that extension in the right ways, we can actually achieve quite a bit in our lives. Throughout this book, I'll dive deeper into that belief, uncovering the science behind it and what it means for our own battles. Though this may all sound too good to be true right now, these strategies have worked for me, and if you give them a shot, I think there's a decent chance they'll work for you as well.

WHY I WROTE THIS BOOK

I wrote this book for countless reasons, the most important of which I'll quickly cover here. The first reason was, quite frankly, because I struggled with anxiety for so long and felt I had a story worth sharing. It's my hope that in sharing that story, I'll be able to help others move past their anxiety faster and less arduously.

When you look at the numbers, it's staggering how large a problem mental health is for America. According to a study published in 2017 in *JAMA Internal Medicine*, a peer-reviewed medical journal, nearly 17% of Americans filled at least one prescription for a psychiatric drug in 2013.[2]

Forthcoming data doesn't make it seem as though usage is dropping either. Anxiety and mental health are major issues for this country.

Medical journals aren't the only outlets discussing this phenomenon these days, either. If you visited an entertainment news website in 2017 or 2018, I'm sure you heard about the deaths of some of the world's most beloved and talented individuals due to battles with mental health. Over the last two years, we lost three of my biggest childhood heroes: Chris Cornell, Chester Bennington, and Tim Bergling.

It goes without saying that suicide and mental health are tightly interwoven. The world is losing too many amazing people due to anxiety and depression, and it's downright heartbreaking. It's the beloved individuals we've lost and all those struggling with mental health issues, including the 17% of Americans filling psychiatric drug prescriptions yearly, for whom I wrote this book.

The second reason is that education around mental health in America is abysmal. In order to get a high school diploma, we go through at least twelve years of formal education. We learn everything from history to math to foreign languages. While these subjects set the foundation for lifelong learning and are obviously important, it infuriates me that during these twelve years, most high school students graduate with little, if any, classroom time dedicated to learning skills that will actually help them lead happy lives. I mean, did anyone ever think that, somewhere along the way, it might be a good idea to teach kids the power of their thoughts and the influence those thoughts have over their well-being? I tend to think not.

One of the biggest challenges we face when it comes to anxiety is we don't always know where it comes from or what causes it. Though mental health is starting to get the attention it deserves in the media, it's still a taboo subject for most of America. This taboo, over the years, has created

[2] Moore, Thomas J., and Donald R. Mattison. "Adult Utilization of Psychiatric Drugs and Differences by Sex, Age, and Race." *JAMA Internal Medicine*, vol. 177, no. 2, 2017, p. 274., doi:10.1001/jamainternmed.2016.7507.

a deficiency of available, empowering information on the subject, even outside of our schooling systems.

As I began my own mental health journey, I didn't know who to reach out to or where to look for help. When I finally started looking with intent, I spent years frustratingly experimenting with strategies that didn't actually help me keep my symptoms at bay. Thus, most of the tactics I cover in this book are ones I developed through trial and error. Since finding effective methods for dealing with anxiety can be difficult, I wanted to put my own in one central place and give those on their own mental health journeys somewhere to turn. That was the third reason for writing this book.

Lastly, I wrote this book because I believe that the methods I've developed to assist me with my own anxiety are subject-agnostic. That is, they can be effective when applied to anything that brings you anxiety, be it an upcoming event, a scary situation, or nagging self-doubt. You may spend hours fretting about how you'll pay your bills this month. I may question whether I'll survive jumping out of a plane next week. The very things that make us anxious aren't all that important in regard to getting out of our heads. What is important is that we develop and leverage the proper tools for doing so on a consistent basis.

These are the very tools we'll cover throughout this book. By the end, it's my hope you'll be able to take some of these tools and build your own anxiety toolkit. With this kit, you'll be equipped to both lower the frequency at which you get yourself into anxious states as well as get yourself out of them quicker when they do arise.

WHO AM I?

So just who am I and why am I qualified to write a book on this subject? Admittedly, I'm not the person you'd probably think of when seeing a book like this. I'm not a doctor. I have no formal medical or mental health training. I'm just a twenty-eight year old man from Massachusetts who's been through some of the same things you have.

I was blessed with two amazing parents, a driven and caring brother, and a childhood of fond memories in a suburb just outside of Boston. I graduated from Boston College in 2012. I've worked in the tech sector for the past six years, and am really just another one of the faces in the crowd. Yet, despite what you might see on the surface, for a good portion of my life, I've struggled with Generalized Anxiety Disorder.

I've been through most of it. The sleepless nights, the panic attacks, the dread, the cold sweats, the heart palpitations. An engineer at heart, I love to figure out why things work the way they do. Throughout this book, you'll see that engineering background come through as I draw parallels between computer systems and how the human mind works.

When I was first diagnosed with anxiety, I promised myself I'd get to the bottom of it. I'd figure it all out and eventually write a book on the strategies I developed to help me overcome. Well, more than ten years later, here we are. I've spent those years, although reluctantly at times, placing myself in the situations that scared me the most. After more than a decade of doing this (sometimes with success, sometimes with failure), I feel I'm finally ready to share some of my experiences and the powerful lessons that came with them.

Almost all of the strategies we'll elaborate upon in this book come directly from my own struggles with anxiety. Though I may not stand out in the crowd or have a medical school diploma on the wall, I think that's the very point. A great number of the people in that crowd silently suffer from anxiety as well. Through that suffering, many of those people have developed battle-tested strategies that work for them. I've done the same, and hope that as I share my tactics, I'll give you a leg up in your own battle.

HOW THIS BOOK IS ORGANIZED

This book is broken into two parts. The first part is all about defining anxiety and developing strategies for getting ourselves out of acute states of it. I'll begin by introducing my *Three Tenets of Anxiety* and explaining how they lay the foundation for the tools and strategies I'll develop later in the book.

From there, I'll introduce you to *The Ten Steps to Getting Out of Your Head* – my framework for moving yourself out of an anxious state. Lastly, to round out the first part of the book, I'll put *The Ten Steps* into action by applying them, one by one, to a common, anxiety-provoking situation, so you can do the same when you find yourself overcome with fear.

While the first part of this book is geared toward overcoming anxiety in the short term, the second part focuses on lowering the frequency at which we experience it in the long run. We'll discuss various strategies we can employ for developing lives of calmness and tranquility. And good news – we won't have to take any tranquilizers to do so.

Some of the topics I'll cover in the second part include coming to view anxiety as a vehicle for personal growth, harnessing the power of a disciplined mind, recognizing the impact our diets can have on our mental health, and seeing that by focusing on something outside of ourselves, we can take back the internal power our anxiety often withholds from us.

My hope is that after you read this book, you'll walk away with effective strategies for managing and overcoming your anxiety, both in the short term and the long term. Not every strategy will resonate with you and that's okay. We all have different triggers for anxiety, so we must also have differing strategies for getting out of our own heads. At the end of the day, what we're all after is a less stressful life full of energy and excitement. It will be my job to show you how to get there and your job to take the necessary action. Now I know you're probably just as excited as I am to begin, so without further ado, let's discuss what anxiety is and where it comes from.

WHAT IS ANXIETY?

In order to most effectively combat anxiety, we must first come to understand what it is. Once we define it, discover how it arises within us, and uncover what its proverbial weaknesses are, we'll be better equipped to slay the dragon, so to speak.

Even though we could put countless different names on it, what anxiety boils down to is fear. It is fear of the unknown, fear of what could happen to us or what could transpire in any of the areas of our lives we deem important. When we're feeling anxious about attending a performance review with our boss or going white water rafting, what we're really feeling is this fear. We're afraid, on some level, the worst possible outcome will occur.[3] We're scared our boss will fire us in front of the whole company or our raft will capsize and we'll seriously injure ourselves.

From the research I've gathered, as well as my own battle with anxiety, I would say this fear is a synergy between two forces: our innate fight-or-flight mechanisms and the looping-thinking we engage in, either consciously or subconsciously, over the things that scare us. Anatomically speaking, it's the battle between the rational and emotional parts of our brains, namely, our prefrontal cortices and limbic systems, including the latter's fear-producing amygdala.[4]

The reason I say anxiety is a synergy is that these two sources often feed off one another and become stronger,

---

[3] Beidel, Deborah C, et al. "Anxiety, Trauma, and Stressor-Related Disorders." *Abnormal Psychology: A Scientist-Practitioner Approach*, 4th ed., Pearson Education, Inc., 2017, pp. 116–117.

[4] Van der Kolk, Bessel A. "Healing From Trauma: Owning Your Self." *The Body Keeps the Score: Brain, Mind, and Body in the Healing of Trauma*, Penguin Books, 2015, pp. 205–207.

which ultimately increases the intensity and duration of our fear. I'll explain both sources of this synergy, in depth, throughout this book, but let's first start by discussing the origins of our fight-or-flight mechanisms with a little trip back in time. Okay, maybe a big trip. Let's flash back to about one million years ago, during the times of Homo erectus, our adventurous ancestor.

For a minute, imagine you're out in the forest, searching for dinner with your forager friends. You pick some fruits and vegetables and are excited to bring your findings back to the tribe for a communal meal. You start thinking about how enjoyable this meal will be, when, out of nowhere, you hear a loud rustle come from one of the bushes next to you. Within an instant, your heart rate skyrockets and your mind races uncontrollably. You look over at your friends. None of them seem concerned. Just a second later, you hear a loud and distinct roar and, without even thinking, immediately drop your strawberries and lettuce and start sprinting.

Before you know it, you're more than a hundred yards away from the madness. While still running at full speed, you look over your shoulder, back at your friends. Holy crap! The rest of the crew is face-to-face with a ferocious, hungry lion. Your stomach sinks. Are they going to make it out alive? You keep running as fast as you can until you make it back to camp. As you attempt to pull yourself out of your panic, you can't help but think, "Why didn't they take off at the first sign of danger as well? Didn't they hear those noises coming from the bushes?"

EVOLUTION'S ROLE IN ANXIETY

Most of us have heard of the concepts of natural selection and evolution. In a nutshell, these theories suggest that over time, traits and behaviors that increase man's odds for survival get passed to more offspring and subsist in the gene pool longer than those that do not. This is where we get the term *survival of the fittest*.

Individuals and bloodlines that possess survival-promoting traits stand a better chance at living long enough to reproduce and pass those traits on to subsequent generations, while those that do not, often die off, taking their traits with them, out of the gene pool. Evolution, then, is the word used to describe the long-term accumulation of these survived traits.[5] As more useful traits are passed on, man morphs and becomes more adapted to his environment.

One of the most powerful traits that has developed along the course of human history is man's ability to respond to potentially threatening stimuli at a moment's notice. This reactionary capability lives within all of us, though is particularly heightened for some, which partially explains why we all experience differing levels of anxiety.[6]

Sure, a rustle in the bushes could just be a harmless chipmunk. But it could also be a lion. It's the ability to perceive the potential threat and take immediate action, when necessary, that likely saved countless numbers of our ancestors. Those that weren't able to react fast enough to such threats often went the way of your hypothetical friends from our story just a minute ago.

Over time, this system of immediate reaction to threats, known as our fight-or-flight response, became one of man's biggest assets.[7] It often made the difference between safely arriving home for dinner and becoming someone else's dinner. As mankind has evolved, so has our ability to perceive potential danger.

Though it's likely our fight-or-flight systems once only reacted to physical threats, they eventually evolved to respond to all other forms of potential danger and pain as well, including that of the mental, spiritual, or emotional

---

[5] Hall, Brian K. "Before Darwin." *Strickberger's Evolution*, edited by Benedikt Hallgrímsson, 4th ed., Jones and Bartlett Publishers, 2007, pp. 4–5.
[6] Whitaker, Robert. "The Benzo Trap." *Anatomy of an Epidemic: Magic Bullets, Psychiatric Drugs, and the Astonishing Rise of Mental Illness in America*, Crown Publishers, 2010, p. 127.
[7] Kozlowska, Kasia. "Fear and the Defense Cascade: Clinical Implications and Management." *Harvard Review of Psychiatry*, 8 July 2015, pp. 263–287., doi:10.1097/HRP.0000000000000065.

type. As time has gone on, our brains have connected the avoidance of potential pain (like being eaten by a lion) to an increased likelihood of survival. The more lions we run away from, the more likely we'll be to carry on our lineage.

One of the challenges we face as modern day humans is that while we don't run into nearly as many lions as we used to, our brains still operate as if that's the case. When faced with self-doubt or placed into important, though non-life-threatening situations, it's not uncommon for us to feel anxious, nervous, or downright dreadful. These feelings are also part of our survival instincts. Our brains flood our bloodstreams with cortisol, the stress hormone, to inspire us to take action quickly and decisively.[8]

Stressful situations we can't immediately flee sometimes cause our cortisol levels to stay elevated for longer periods of time. When we find ourselves in these situations, we often have no idea what to do. We don't want our fears to come to life, nor do we want to endure the dreadful feelings associated with the release of our stress hormones. However, since we can't do anything to control either undesirable experience, we often find ourselves stuck worrying about both our fears and our reactions to them. This makes us feel helpless and causes us to react with even more fear, which, in turn, augments the anxiety synergy further.

The reason for all of this stems back to our evolution. Our brains are wired to survive.[9] Anything that could potentially cause us pain is something our brains want to avoid, and the release of cortisol helps us do just that. But when there's nothing in front of us to fight with or run from, it feels like there's a missing link to this equation. That's because there is.

Though fight-or-flight responses and elevated levels of cortisol may be our body's default reactions to stress, they

---

[8] Lee, Do Yup, et al. "Technical and Clinical Aspects of Cortisol as a Biochemical Marker of Chronic Stress." *BMB Reports*, vol. 48, no. 4, Apr. 2015, pp. 209–216., doi:10.5483/BMBRep.2015.48.4.275.
[9] Van der Kolk, Bessel A. "Running For Your Life: The Anatomy of Survival." *The Body Keeps the Score: Brain, Mind, and Body in the Healing of Trauma*, Penguin Books, 2015, p. 55.

can actually hinder us in situations like the ones I'm describing. In order to lower the intensity of these innate reactions, we need to leverage the other side of the anxiety synergy. That is, we must break out of the fear-based thoughts that often accompany these fight-or-flight responses.

THOUGHTS ARE THINGS

If you've ever tried to think your way out of your anxiety, I'd guess you probably found it only made things worse. This is because trying to reason your way out of your head leads to looping-thinking. It's a frustrating process, and it's one of the main reasons, if not the main reason, we stay stuck in anxious states. I call it looping-thinking rather than logic because it doesn't get you anywhere.

The process typically goes a bit like this: you think about something that scares you, which makes you feel, well, scared. You try to rationalize why this thing shouldn't or won't scare you, which, counterintuitively, only makes you feel even worse or more scared. This increased sense of fear results in a heightened state within your body, which you experience through *anxious symptoms*, such as sweaty palms, heart palpitations, or butterflies in your stomach.

This heightened state, in turn, makes you feel like you need to combat the fear even more, which only propels you to turn the thoughts over in your mind yet again. There are only a few ways this looping-thinking ends:

1. You become so exhausted by your fear and its effect on your body that you give up
2. You make the realization that your thinking, not the object of your fear itself, is making you anxious
3. Something comes along that distracts you out of your loop

Regardless of how the thinking ends, you never solve the fear that pushes you to spin the wheels in your mind. To be honest, I'm not sure you can. The only thing that has ever worked for me has been to drop the thoughts creating the fear in the first place.

There's a vital premise behind this process and it's the concept that thoughts are things. They aren't just abstract concepts or meaningless inhabitants of our minds. They're carriers of chemical messages that influence how we feel.[10] They have the capacity to both create anxious symptoms and turn on our fight-or-flight responses. When you think about really good things or really bad things for a long time, those thoughts affect how you feel on both a mental and physical level. Don't believe me? Just sit down and try it for yourself.

The reason this premise is so important is our thoughts influence the intensity of our physical symptoms and fight-or-flight responses, and both our thoughts and our biological reactions lead to the phenomenon we call anxiety. Thus, if we're able to control our thoughts, or at the very least, stop ourselves from entering patterns of looping-thinking so easily, we can influence how much anxiety we experience. Since anxiety is a synergy, we'll experience less of it, in disproportionate fashion, to the extent that we improve our ability to control our thoughts. It goes without saying that this is no easy task. Seriously. It's really freaking hard. But if we want to develop a life of inner peace, it's something we absolutely must do.

Now I don't want to mislead you into believing you can permanently turn off your fight-or-flight system through your thinking. That would be a very tall order, and, I'd argue, is probably not what you actually want. Not getting excited every once in a while can be just as harmful as anxiety is, in regard to both your physical health and well-being. You can, however, learn to *influence* your body's automatic responses quite a bit, and train yourself to be less

---

[10] Amen, Daniel G. "Enhancing Positive Thought Patterns and Strengthening Connections: Deep Limbic System Prescriptions." Change Your Brain, Change Your Life: The Breakthrough Program for Conquering Anxiety, Depression, Obsessiveness, Anger, and Impulsiveness, Three Rivers Press, 1998, pp. 55–57.

reactive to the everyday situations you face that are frightening, albeit, relatively harmless.

When I talk about control versus influence, what I mean is that we might not ever know for certain our hearts won't race while giving an important presentation to our classmates. However, we can know that the less we engage in looping-thinking over the presentation before it arrives, the less our hearts will race when we ultimately stand up in front of the classroom. Though this may sound slightly disappointing or disheartening at first, there's actually more to it than meets the eye.

The symptoms of our fight-or-flight reactions often cause us to become even more fearful. We get up in front of that classroom, feel our hearts pounding, and think, "Oh my god, why is this happening?" which only makes us more scared and intensifies our butterflies or racing hearts. Though we can never guarantee such a response won't be present, we can most certainly lower that response through disciplined thinking. And with a lowered biological response in the heat of the moment, we'll find the accompanying thoughts less intense, which usually serves to alleviate us of our symptoms faster.

This is something we'll cover in more detail in a later chapter, *We Determine What Anxiety Means.* For now, just knowing that our thoughts and biological reactions work in tandem helps us, even if only to a small degree, avoid the patterns that lead to anxiety in the first place. As we'll see, this, and not the lack of a heightened physical reaction, is actually what we're looking for.

I would imagine none of this comes off as rocket science. It seems like fairly common sense to say that if you think about negative things all the time, you're probably going to feel pretty terrible. Even though that may be the case, it's clear that most of us, while deeming these concepts obvious, aren't practicing them. If we were, we wouldn't be wrestling with our mental demons so much. This gap between theory and practice is actually one of the most difficult parts of dealing with anxiety, and is what we'll spend much of this book discussing.

THE THREE TENETS OF ANXIETY

It's not enough to merely know what anxiety is and where it comes from. We also need to know why we enter patterns of looping-thinking when they almost never move us away from our fears. Once we're armed with answers to these sorts of *why* questions, we can develop strategies that push us out of our default thought patterns and into ones that promote inner calm. Let's begin answering those *why* questions now, as we set the stage for strategy development throughout the rest of this book. I present to you *The Three Tenets of Anxiety* – what I like to think of as the mental health version of Newton's three laws of motion.

The first tenet states that **all anxiety is rooted in uncertainty**.[11] Can you think of a time you felt anxious about something good that was 100% likely to happen? I imagine you'd have a difficult time doing so. Like we've discussed, anxiety stems from a survival mechanism we developed over millions of years. It's meant to help us avoid situations and possibilities that could cause us pain. When we know what's going to happen, and view that happenstance as a good thing, there isn't much for our brains to worry about.

It's only in situations where we don't know what the outcome will be that our brains sometimes start getting us ready for the worst possible scenarios. The more important and uncertain an event or possibility is to us, the more our

---

[11] Ladouceur, R., Dugas, M. J., Freeston, M. H., Léger, E., Gagnon, F., & Thibodeau, N. (2000). Efficacy of a cognitive–behavioral treatment for generalized anxiety disorder: Evaluation in a controlled clinical trial. *Journal of Consulting and Clinical Psychology, 68*(6), 957-964, doi:10.1037/0022-006X.68.6.957.

bodies alert us to the potential pain it could cause us. For example, jumping out of an airplane is a monumental and uncertain thing. If the jump goes poorly, we could sustain serious injuries or even die. To our brains, this potential pain is seen as much more likely, and much more impactful, than performing an *indoor* skydive.

It's this uncertainty that becomes the basis for our anxiety. If we knew with 100% certainty our parachutes would deploy and we'd successfully survive our skydives, there would be nothing to worry about. Sure, very few events in our lives come with such a guarantee, but the fact remains that the more likely a neutral or positive outcome is to occur, the less likely we are to worry about it. This is an important distinction to make, for as we'll see in a later chapter, this uncertainty is something we can influence to a degree.

The second tenet states that **the more you delve into your anxiety, the worse it becomes**. This should come as a refresher after our introduction to looping-thinking. When we find ourselves in the grips of frightening situations, our brains go on high alert. They see uncertainty and want to know, right away, how things will ultimately turn out. In an effort to remove this uncertainty, our minds gravitate toward the kind of obsessive, endless thinking we've already discussed.

I'm sure you've taken part in this type of thinking before. It's terrible. It makes you feel as if your brain has been hijacked. In these thought patterns, it's extremely difficult to think about anything other than the thing scaring you. Our brains perform this mental hijacking because they hate uncertainty and equate it, often, with death. Even though the event or situation representing the uncertainty might be days or weeks away, our brains don't want to wait for death. They want to confront and stomp it out right now.

The problem with this mental commandeering is that it's not productive. We can push back against our self-doubts or try to picture ourselves in upcoming, scary situations, doing the very things we're afraid of over and over again, and the result will always be the same. Such strategies will never actually quell our fears around the very things making us anxious.

When we engage in this kind of thinking, we signal to our brains that the things scaring us really are important and prove to ourselves just how impossible it is to know how things will play out. Yet still we go, like mad men, proverbially thinking ourselves into oblivion. Even though refusing to give in to patterns of looping-thinking is one of the hardest things to do when it comes to anxiety, it's exactly what we must do, as this is how we stop fear in its tracks. If you take nothing else away from this book, I hope it's this concept.

I know when I start to feel a little anxious, I have a propensity to try and reason my way out of it. If I'm feeling nervous about attending a networking event, I sometimes try to visualize myself at the event, talking to people and shaking hands while *not* being nervous. I apply logic to the situation in an effort to convince myself that when I'm actually at the event, I won't be anxious.

This kind of mental rehearsal is rarely effective for me. I could sit in my room all day and try to envision something not happening (not being anxious, not being nervous) but all I would ever get is more of what I'm looking to avoid. The object of your focus becomes your experience, whether you're trying to avert it or bring it to life. The more you look into the abyss, the more the abyss looks back into you.[12] This brings me to the third and final tenet of anxiety.

The third tenet states that **you cannot solve your anxiety; the only way past it is to put it down entirely and decide not to fight with it**. Let me ask you a question. Have you ever done something slightly scary without being anxious about it and then retroactively gone back and questioned why you weren't scared while doing it? Have you ever then become anxious about going through the situation again, even though you'd already been through it once successfully? I know I have.

---

[12] Nietzsche, Friedrich W. "Aphorism 146." *Beyond Good and Evil : Prelude to a Philosophy of the Future*, Penguin Books, 1990.

THE THREE TENETS OF ANXIETY

When I first joined my previous employer, I got accustomed to the fact that we had one-on-ones with our managers every week. At first, I didn't think twice about these meetings. They were just times to catch up and see how things were going. A few months into my stint at the company, however, I grew fearful of them. I came to see them as planned ways for my manager to criticize my work or reprimand me, even though I had never been reprimanded during one. My worry over these one-one-ones quickly expanded into full-blown anxiety. In turn, I went on the defensive, plotting all the ways I could outwit or defeat my fear. Sadly, the harder I wrestled with it, the more it proliferated.

After a few days of fighting this fear at my desk, I went for a walk. I took several deep breaths in order to slow my mind down enough to think clearly. As I broke out of my looping-thinking, I remembered a key insight I had drawn from so many previous anxious situations – it was my pushing back against the fear, my insistence on solving it, that kept me stressed and anxious. At that moment, I saw no other way out but to stop focusing on and fighting that fear. Once I did that, it finally dissipated.

This counterintuitive kind of reasoning is very hard to uncover when our worries take over most of our mental capacities, leaving us wrapped up in our heads. But that doesn't mean we shouldn't continually remind ourselves of this lesson. Fear is an emotion. When we focus on our emotions, they grow. We can't solve our fear, but we can cut off its energy source by taking our focus off it. When we apply this concept, even in the scariest of situations, we will almost always find our worries retreating.

EXACTLY WHAT *NOT* TO DO

In September of 2013, I signed up to go skydiving. Immediately upon making my reservation, I was ecstatic. Skydiving was on my bucket list, and I couldn't wait to experience it. Then, a few days later, I told some colleagues about my upcoming jump.

"Oh wow. I would never do that. Way too risky," replied one of my friends. "What happens if your chute doesn't deploy? How scary would it be to just plummet to your death?" asked another.

Holy shit. What *would* happen if my chute didn't deploy? I simply hadn't been too concerned about that earlier. Yet after that conversation, with so much negative feedback from my peers, it was difficult to look at the dive in the same fashion.

As soon as I got home, a sense of dread came over me. What seemed like an awesome experience just an hour prior had quickly transformed into a bit of a nightmare. No longer was I excited to freefall through the sky – I was petrified. My brain had picked up on the newly perceived risk of the jump and identified it as a potential source of pain (this time, death, literally). Once my brain sensed this potential pain, my fight-or-flight system kicked into overdrive. My heart raced out of my chest, even though my jump was still over a week away.

In that moment, I had a choice. I could've engaged the fear-based energy coursing through my body or let it be. I could've let that energy catapult me into full-blown anxiety or chosen to guard my thoughts and accept the fact that this upcoming adventure had some large risks associated with it. Unfortunately, at the time, I didn't know as much about anxiety as I do now, so I wasn't able to come to this realization. As such, I subconsciously chose to follow my anxious energy into the depths of hell. The next several days were a disaster, to say the least.

For days on end, I incessantly pictured myself jumping out of the plane. My logic was if I could find a way to visualize myself successfully ripping through the skies, then I could calm myself down and eventually make the jump with ease. I didn't know it at the time, but this was, quite literally, the definition of rumination – rehashing your troubles endlessly and dragging yourself deeper into madness while convincing yourself that you're near an epiphany.[13]

---

[13] Blackburn, Elizabeth, and Elissa Epel. "Mind Your Telomeres: Negative

The more I tried to picture myself on the edge of the plane or in the sky, the more anxious I felt. First came a thought of not being able to catch the wind and flailing dreadfully through the clouds. Next came thoughts of perishing on my jump and my family getting the news that I didn't make it. These visions gripped me as I spiraled deeper into my head and the anxiety itself.

The day before the jump was surreal. I honestly felt like I was barely alive. I was just a disembodied head, so wrapped up in my fears that I couldn't bring myself to think about anything else. My family tried talking to me but I couldn't form more than a few abbreviated sentences. I was so focused on the dive, I couldn't divert my attention from it.

Trapped in my head, I spent most of the day in my room, running through the situation endlessly. I cut myself off from the world, reasoning that in just a few more minutes, I'd think myself out of the problem and be home free. Boy, how stupid that sounds now, looking back. I'd just spent the past several days trying to do that very thing and failed miserably.

I went to bed that night in sheer horror of the next day. I was going to make the jump anyway, I told myself. When I woke up that next morning, I saw a text message on my phone. "Your jump has been cancelled due to cloud coverage." Sweet baby Jesus! It was a miracle! Immediately, I felt my fears melt away. I ran downstairs in jubilation like I'd just won the lottery. I was so happy to be out of the mess. Sure, I handled the entire situation extremely poorly, but at least it was over. It was an amazing feeling.

The tactics I employed in the days leading up to my skydive were some of the least empowering or effective strategies I could've ever drawn up. The reason I told this story was not to scare you or make you feel like you can't get out of anxious situations yourself, but to show you how dangerous it is to get in your head and try to battle your fears. In the chapter after next, we'll finally begin

Thinking, Resilient Thinking." *The Telomere Effect*, Grand Central Publishing, 2017, p. 107.

developing strategies you can use in situations like my skydiving preparation to help get yourself back to calm. But first, there's one more crucial topic we must cover.

STATE MANAGEMENT

When we find ourselves in important, uncertain situations, our bodies naturally identify these situations as threats and ready our fight-or-flight response systems. As referenced in my lion-chasing story earlier, this reaction stems from survival instincts. Important, uncertain situations and what-ifs have the ability to bring us pain. Something like not getting into our dream college is an emotionally taxing process that our brains, naturally, would prefer to avoid.

On a grand scale, our brains equate large amounts of pain with death. Since the brain is wired for survival, it's equally and oppositely wired to avoid anything that could cause such pain and lead toward our demise. A first date or the thought that you might not accomplish an important goal you set for yourself, while not inherently dangerous, can throw up all sorts of red flags for our brains, signaling that potential pain is right around the corner. When our brains detect this potential pain, they move into higher gears that help us combat the unease or run from it altogether.

It's at the point of fight-or-flight activation that many folks might say their anxiety kicks in. However, this activation is only part of the overall feeling that we've come to know as anxiety. When our hearts race or our stomachs turn, it's easy to give in to the chaos and set off a chain of destructive thoughts, further intensifying our fear. But that chain of thought does not simply come from out of the blue. We are responsible for setting that thought train in motion. And most of us, in fact, set that train off long before our fight-or-flight systems kick in.

To illustrate my point, I'd like to introduce a concept called *state management*. The term has its roots in the field of computer science, and, well, I'm a bit of a computer nerd, so I've adopted it myself. I love drawing parallels between writing software and modeling human behavior, and state management is one of the concepts in computer programming that helps me do so easily. If computer science isn't your thing, not to worry. I'll keep the discussion high-level and to the point so we can relate it back to anxiety quickly and effectively.

As it relates to software, state management is the term that describes how a computer program updates itself as it receives or observes user inputs, new data entries, and the like. An example of this concept in action is how a website manages and updates its user interface (its layout, buttons, and text fields, for example) as a visitor clicks or types on the site.

While a user tries to log in to the website, the site might keep its login button disabled until he or she has entered both a valid username and password. Doing so informs the user that he or she must take more action before moving forward. Once the user enters the right information, the website changes the state of its login button by making it clickable, allowing the user to submit his or her credentials.

The most important premise of state management is that software programs must actively watch out for and determine when they should change the state of any of the elements they control. Even though it might sound like this has nothing to do with anxiety, there's a greater parallel than you might see on the surface. Just like computer systems change states with great frequency, we are constantly entering and leaving states of differing levels of anxiety. This is precisely why we feel fearful sometimes, but not all the time.

So much of our experience of anxiety, then, is the degree to which we're able to manage our own internal state. When we feel fear or worry building inside us and respond to those feelings appropriately, we lower the odds that they'll send us into extreme states that are harder to get out of.

Of course, knowing exactly how to respond to fear is paramount. Strategies such as listening to a favorite song, going for a walk, or using a deep-breathing technique are just a few of the potential, powerful ways we can redirect our worries. We'll cover methods like these in the following chapter. For now, let's focus on setting the foundation. Let's embrace the idea that getting ourselves back to positive states when we're feeling fearful is our job. Without buying into this concept, we'll continue to overlook our own power and ignore such rechanneling strategies.

If it sounds like what I'm advocating is a practice in self-awareness, that's because it is.[14] Conditioning ourselves to regularly observe shifts in how we feel helps us get out of states that don't serve us. As we become more aware, we'll act more like well-written software programs – on the lookout for changes in our internal and external environments, ready to move ourselves to more empowering states at a moment's notice.

One specific area in which this concept is particularly relevant is that of panic attacks. Having suffered a couple of them myself, I've come to learn, firsthand, how closely linked poor state management is with acute trepidation. Whenever I talk to folks who are struggling with panic attacks in their own lives, I remind them that even though it feels like these attacks come out of nowhere, they almost always arise from an anxious state. That is, even though the accompanying symptoms intensify quickly during an attack, panic gains its momentum in the days, hours, or minutes prior as we shift our thinking to the negative and put ourselves on high alert.

Thus, if we want to experience fewer anxious symptoms and panic attacks, we need to figure out how to both get into anxious states less often as well as get ourselves out of them once they've arrived. While the concept of state management is a vital part of that process, it's more the *what* than it is the *how*. Just knowing we need

---

[14] Van der Kolk, Bessel A. "Healing From Trauma: Owning Your Self." *The Body Keeps the Score: Brain, Mind, and Body in the Healing of Trauma*, Penguin Books, 2015, pp. 210–212.

to constantly monitor our state doesn't give us the strategies for doing so. To launch us toward developing all of those *hows*, I'd like to introduce one other vital computer programming concept, *the state machine*.

THE STATE MACHINE

Now that we know what state management is, understanding what a state machine is shouldn't be too complicated. If state management is the concept of observing inputs in order to move to the right states at the right time, then a state machine is the map that details all of those possible states. That is, it outlines all the ways a system could get into and out of all of its potential configurations as well as how it behaves in each of those configurations.[15] Now, I'm sure that still doesn't make a hell of a lot of sense, so I'll explain it with a more real-life example.

Let's say we want to create a software program that models a laptop computer. If we were to write a state machine representing the laptop, it might have a few states, such as out-of-battery, off, asleep, and active. As a user engages with his or her laptop, he or she supplies inputs to the system. These inputs could come in many forms, including plugging in the power cord, opening the laptop, pressing the power button, or typing on the keyboard.

The fashion in which our software model responds to these inputs is dependent upon its current state. For example, if a user logs a keystroke while the laptop is turned off, our model won't do anything. However, if he or she does so while the computer is on, our model might put that keystroke on the screen, depending on what program is open.

To move between states, certain inputs are required at the right time. For example, for our system to move to the turned off state, a user must press the power button on a

---

[15] Kent, Allen, and James G Williams. "Finite-State Machines." *Encyclopedia of Computer Science and Technology*, vol. 25, CRC Press, 1991, pp. 73–78.

laptop that's turned on, or start charging a laptop that's out of battery. If the user presses the power button while his or her laptop is out of juice, it will stay in the out-of-battery state.

This high-level picture of the state machine is where our current foray into computer programming will end. We now have all the theoretical knowledge required to link back to our own internal battles. The reason the state machine is so important in our day-to-day experience of anxiety is that it illustrates that moving from one internal state to the next requires the right actions at the right time. For example, moving from a worried state to a joyful state requires different inputs than moving from a worried state to a hopeless state. Determining the inputs required for moving out of fearful states, then, is our next vital task, since doing so will give us a framework for escaping our anxiety when we dance with it most closely.

When we're in such powerful, anxious states, we have a tendency to overthink. The problem with this overthinking is it doesn't help us move to a different state, such as tranquility. It just keeps us where we are. Moreover, in these fearful states, we typically experience negative feelings such as dread, despair, or doubt. These feelings further influence our behavior, typically propelling us back into more cycles of overthinking or worrying about when our next anxious symptom will pop up.

So often we look at upcoming events that frighten us and think that being in said events is what makes us anxious, not realizing that so much of the anxiety we feel in these situations is brought on by poor state management well in advance of them. That is, we get into our heads over these events before they arrive and put ourselves in states of fear that we don't leave until after they've come to pass. Getting out of such states is paramount to avoiding so much of the despair we associate with anxiety in general.

While this theoretical talk is important and certainly sets the foundation for more practical learning, it's not something we can directly put into practice. We could talk about state machines all day, but if we don't know what actions to take when we enter our anxious states, we likely won't be any better off at managing our anxiety overall. Luckily, discussing such tactics is where we're headed next. In the following chapter, I'll present my *Ten Steps to Getting Out of Your Head* – the ten most effective strategies I've developed for getting myself out of my own anxious states.

Think of these strategies as the missing inputs to your anxiety state machine – the ones required for moving yourself out of stress and back to calm. Now that we've covered the theory behind state management, these inputs should make a bit more sense. These same steps have been instrumental in my own battles, and I hope you find the same for yourself.

THE TEN STEPS TO GETTING OUT OF YOUR HEAD

A few summers ago, I fortuitously ran into an old classmate of mine, Tess, at the bar. We were in similar friend circles in school but had never really hung out. I always thought she was really attractive, so when I ran into her, I seized the opportunity. I asked for her phone number and invited her out for drinks that next week. She said yes. It was a very exciting moment for me.

We went out a few days later and hit it off. There was just one problem. She was heading out of the country on a three-month-long vacation the following week. We made plans to hang out again before she left. I almost cancelled that second date. I had trouble justifying investing in a potential relationship with her leaving the country in just a few days. But at the last second, I came to my senses and decided I'd be a fool to not go.

We celebrated her birthday with a bunch of her friends and stayed out pretty late despite it being a work night. We were having too much fun laughing and dancing to care. I woke up the next morning feeling great. Then I remembered how fleeting it all was. She'd be leaving town in less than two days to prepare for her trip and then would be out of the country for three months. My excitement soon faded.

We texted each other and mentioned how unfortunate the timing was. I was glad we'd run into each other, but still, I had to wonder what would've happened if we'd crossed paths the year before. She took off on her vacation and I promised myself I'd let it go. It didn't make sense to hold myself back in the dating realm while she was out of town. But, to my surprise, we stayed in touch, and over the next few weeks, our feelings seemed to grow stronger toward one another. It would be a long time until she returned, but, there was something there, and I wanted to see where it might go.

As the weeks wore on, I grew anxious over the situation. I realized I was in deeper than I wanted to be. I mean I really liked this woman that I'd only been out with twice. That fact alone scared me quite a bit. Moreover, it seemed like every time I opened Snapchat or Instagram, she was at the top of my feed, posing with a new guy she'd met on her journey. These pictures incited a slew of fearful thoughts in my mind, including her dating one of these guys or staying in Europe permanently. In an attempt to avoid these thoughts, I used social media less frequently that summer, even though it wasn't always easy to do so.

Back in the states, I was working as a consultant on a software project for a large company in Boston. That company hired my team somewhat quickly. They really wanted to work with us, but didn't have much for us to do right away. They were afraid that if they waited, we might get booked by a different client, so they signed us on and said they'd try to pull some work together for us.

The first several weeks of the project were a drag. My team and I sat at our desks and listened to podcasts, pretending to be busy. We were not. My boredom with the project only made the situation with Tess, and my anxiety around it, that much worse.

Right in the middle of her time being away, I put myself into an anxious funk by dwelling on whether or not things would work out between us. Visions of my previous panic attack with Monica haunted me and made me feel like

I was destined to have one in front of Tess when she got back. I fought these thoughts and tried to visualize myself *not* having a nervous breakdown while out with her, but got absolutely nowhere. I convinced myself I was close to thinking my way through the anxiety, unaware of the fact that, by constantly chewing it over, I was actually making it even worse.

Days later, sitting in my client's office, I had an epiphany. It's a day I'll never forget. As I looked out the window at the city of Boston, I said to myself, "I've been spinning these thoughts over incessantly for the last few weeks. It's not getting me anywhere good. This is complete insanity. I need to stop it."

I'd been through similar anxious situations countless times before. Sure, the outcome of this situation was pretty important to me, but so too were all those other experiences, at least seemingly, at the time. In that moment, I knew the only way to regain my sanity would be to get out of my head and stop ruminating over whether it would work out with Tess. It would be no easy task, but it was what I needed to do.

Riding the wave of this epiphany, I pulled out my phone. I felt charged with some sort of creative energy and wanted to capture it. I opened the Notes application on my phone and typed as quickly as I could. I titled this brain dump *Anxiety Strategies*. I honestly didn't even know what I was doing. I was just trying to pour out my thoughts and make myself feel better. But I kept writing. When I was finally out of ideas, I read what I had created. It was a list of tactics for getting out of my head and moving myself out of anxious states. Every day, for the rest of that summer, I practiced those strategies until they became second nature.

With a bit of refinement over the years, those strategies became my *Ten Steps To Getting Out of Your Head*. Each step is spelled out below. I'll explain each one in detail in the following chapters as we begin to put our theoretical discussion into practice.

1. Breathe

2. Determine the true importance of what's making you anxious
3. Evaluate the potential outcomes and reconnect to the one you want
4. Shift your focus to something positive
5. Recite a powerful mantra
6. Stop questioning yourself
7. Utilize an empowering way to feel good, right now
8. Get back to the present moment
9. Remind yourself the worst part of anxiety is the waiting
10. Remember this too shall pass

To this day, I still use these steps every time I find myself in an anxious state. Whether I'm questioning my abilities, waiting for an important date, or anticipating a jump out of an airplane, these are the steps I walk through to calm myself down and put things in perspective. These steps have guided me through countless frightening situations, including when Tess came back from her vacation and we went on a couple of dates.

In the end, it didn't work out between us, but that's the smaller story here. Though I did not get the girl, I got a framework for managing my anxiety that I desperately needed. My hope is this framework will soon become an even bigger story as my readers use it to make strides in their own lives.

I now invite you to delve into *The Ten Steps to Getting Out of Your Head*. I ask that you fully consider each step and try to relate it to your battle. Once you have an understanding of each step, come back to this list and commit it to memory. Carry it on an index card in your pocket, make a poster out of it and hang it on your wall, or make it the background of your computer. Do whatever you need to do to make the steps that work for you a habit. The more you practice them and integrate them into your daily life, the quicker you'll feel their effects.

STEP ONE

Breathe

For a moment, let's pretend you're at a rock climbing gym for the first time. Climbing is a hobby you've always wanted to get into, but have previously found too scary. Your friends were finally able to convince you to go, however, so here you are. You get to the main room of the gym, put on your harness, and look up at the wall in front of you. Next, you attach the climbing rope to your harness and begin to scale the wall. You start moving along just fine, despite the first-climb jitters.

You can't believe how quickly time is going by. It feels like you're racing up the wall. This is the most fun you've had in months. But then, out of nowhere, one of your friends back on the ground yells, "Hey, don't look down!" Unfortunately, you do. In an instant, your connection with the wall disappears. All you can think of is what would happen if you fell. Your heart and mind race uncontrollably as your focus fades. You can't think clearly amongst the plethora of scary thoughts. "Holy shit, why did I think I could do this? This is so freaking scary!"

This transition of going from blissful, carefree climbing to anxiety-riddled paralysis is the epitome of getting in our heads. We go from performing a task without even realizing it, to questioning how we could have possibly just done said thing. With this questioning typically comes a powerful sense of fear – one that often hinders our mental and physical capacities.

This fear doesn't care whether the dangers dancing in your mind are real or just perceived to be real. When you're on the climbing wall with your heart racing, everything seems real. The interesting thing, however, is that as you freak out on the wall, you forget you're securely harnessed to the ceiling, wearing a helmet, and actually only fifteen feet off the ground. And, should your professional-grade harness somehow fail, there's still a heavily padded area on the ground to cushion your fall.

The only problem is, in your state of panic, it's almost impossible to recover such reassuring thoughts. Try as you might, all you can manage to think about is being the first person in the history of the rock climbing gym to die of fear mid-climb. In order to access the type of rational, grounded thoughts I outlined just a second ago, you're going to need to get your body back to calm. You'll do that by breathing.

THE AUTONOMIC NERVOUS SYSTEM

To understand the effect breathing has on our physical symptoms, we need to first discuss the body's autonomic nervous system, often referred to as the ANS, and its substructures. The ANS is a division of our peripheral nervous system, and its role is to regulate primarily involuntary functions of the body, such as digestion and heart rate. If you've ever wondered how you're able to keep breathing while you sleep, the answer is this regulating system.

The autonomic nervous system is broken into two parts, the sympathetic nervous system, the SNS, and the parasympathetic nervous system, the PSNS. Throughout this book, I've made many references to the body's fight-or-flight system. That very system is actually the sympathetic nervous system. It's the one that alerts us to potential threats and helps us move away from them.

The body strives to maintain homeostasis. Being on high alert all the time would be very taxing on our bodies and would prevent us from living normal lives. This is exactly why our parasympathetic nervous system exists. Its main role is to bring the body back to rest after periods of demand and stress. It's often labeled as the system that helps us both feed and breed as well as rest and digest.[16]

---

[16] McCorry, Laurie K. "Physiology of the Autonomic Nervous System."

These two divisions of the ANS work in push and pull fashion. The SNS pushes us into high alert during times of threat and the PSNS pulls us back to calm after the threat has passed. Though these systems can, and mostly do, operate on their own, we can also influence them with our thoughts and behaviors. We saw how this worked already when we discussed how our looping-thinking over the things that scare us activates our fight-or-flight systems.

What we haven't yet talked about is how we can activate our parasympathetic nervous systems to help get us back to calm from panic states sooner. Though there are several different ways we can go about achieving this, the easiest and most accessible is by breathing fully and deeply.[17]

When we enter states of fear, we often hyperventilate. That is, we breathe really fast and feel like we can't catch our breath. There's a reason we feel this way. When we breathe normally, we engage our sympathetic nervous systems as we inhale, temporarily speeding our bodies up, and engage our parasympathetic nervous systems as we exhale, slowing our bodies down.[18] However, when we don't inhale fully and deeply, we can't exhale deeply either. And when we don't exhale fully and deeply, we prevent the PSNS from doing its job sooner, which keeps us revved up and out of breath for longer than we should be.

BREATHE INTO AWARENESS

It's only when our parasympathetic nervous systems re-engage in times of fight-or-flight that we can finally think clearly again. When our thoughts are moving a million miles

American Journal of Pharmaceutical Education, vol. 71, no. 4, 15 Aug. 2007, doi:10.5688/aj710478.

[17] Brown, Richard P, and Patricia L Gerbarg. "Sudarshan Kriya Yogic Breathing in the Treatment of Stress, Anxiety, and Depression: Part II— Clinical Applications and Guidelines." *The Journal of Alternative and Complementary Medicine*, vol. 11, no. 4, 2005, doi:10.1089/acm.2005.11.711.

[18] Van der Kolk, Bessel A. "Brain-Body Connections." *The Body Keeps the Score: Brain, Mind, and Body in the healing of Trauma*, Penguin Books, 2015, p. 79.

a minute, it's very difficult for us to employ logic. This is by design – logic is not a core feature of the sympathetic nervous system. And it's with good reason. If you stopped to think when someone ran after you with a weapon, your pause could give your assailant enough time to reach you.

Not all of the situations that scare us are inherently dangerous, however. Case in point being safely harnessed to a rock climbing wall or worrying about missing your train home. When you find yourself in situations like these, the first thing you need to do is start breathing slowly and deeply, so your stomach, not your chest, rises and falls. Don't be afraid to exaggerate the breathing – whatever it takes to help keep your mind on it. This will engage your parasympathetic nervous system which will, simultaneously, slow down the fight-or-flight system.

The reason this kind of breathing is so important is that activating your body's innate calming abilities gets you back to the place where awareness and logic live quicker, and awareness and logic help you realize when you're engaging in destructive thought patterns. You could tape my *Ten Steps* to your arm and read them everywhere you go, but if you don't first slow yourself down with proper breathing during times of stress, you may never realize you've gotten into your head in the first place. Not making this realization, in turn, might prevent you from carrying out the rest of the steps in the list and keep you stuck in your state of fear longer.

STEP TWO

Determine the true importance of what's making you anxious

In an anxious state, we often get so wrapped up in our thoughts that the very thing making us fearful feels like it's the only important thing in our lives. Most of the time, this is an illusion. Sure, there are the occasional instances where our lives, or something else of true importance, are actually on the line. Let's leave those instances for another time and instead talk about what most of us ruminate over – frightening potential outcomes that seem critical today, but aren't all that important in the grand scheme of things.

After my epiphany in the middle of Tess's vacation, I realized just how well this second step related to the situation in which I found myself. During the previous several weeks, I had gotten so far inside my head about how things would work out with her that it felt like the situation was the only thing that mattered in my life. The rational part of me knew this couldn't be true, but the anxious, emotional part of me argued the opposite. I knew I needed to get some perspective on this dichotomy, so I ran a small thought exercise that I hoped would help me do just that.

I started by taking inventory of everything I thought to be important to me. *My health, my friends, my family, my education, my drive, my financial status, my great memories, the fact that I live in an amazing city, and Tess.* When I sat down and analyzed this list, I realized that while I was temporarily making Tess a top priority, she wasn't actually as important to me as many of the other items I'd brainstormed. By thinking she was, I had deluded myself into feeling that things not working out with her would be a devastating blow.

Let me explain. I'm not saying she wasn't important. I really liked her and thought we had a special connection. It's just that I'd taken the uncertain situation and dumped so much fuel on the fire that I tricked myself into believing she was priority number one. Sure, I'd be disappointed if it didn't work out between us, but not nearly as crushed as if something happened to my friends or family. Putting it in perspective, I thought to myself, "There are literally billions of other women out there. Many of them could provide a similar connection to Tess. There's no replacing your health or your family, however. Those come first."

In most of our anxious states, we follow this same pattern. We get so fixated on one outcome or priority and build it up as this be-all-end-all force in our lives. When we elevate the importance of said outcome past its true importance, we lose sight of our actual priorities and drive ourselves crazy. In reality, the outcome of the situation is often not nearly as important or scary as we're making it out to be. For example, if we totally botch a date, it could suck in the moment, but all we have to do to bounce back is get on a dating app and find one of the many eligible folks nearby to go out with.

One way I test the true importance of something is by asking myself if what I'm worried about will even matter in a year. This is how I distinguish the trivial from the vital. I asked myself this same question in regard to the situation with Tess and realized that if things didn't work out between us, it would probably matter to me in three months, but most likely not twelve. Coming to this conclusion helped me realize the true order of my priorities in life as well as turn down the fear surrounding the outcome. Sure, I was still nervous things might not work out between us, but thanks to this question and answer process, I knew I had far less to fear than my mind was telling me I did.

This is the same kind of thinking I want you to engage in when you find yourself in a heightened, anxious state. Start by brainstorming what's important to you, then see where the situation or idea in front of you ranks on that list. Once you have that answer, ask yourself how you'd feel in one year if you were to lose each item on your list. Often, this brainstorming activity can help pull you out of your head by showing you that the very thing making you anxious is not as important as you're making it out to be. Apply this kind of thinking at the peak of your anxious states, and I think you'll quickly discover a better perspective on your fears.

STEP THREE

Evaluate the potential outcomes and reconnect to the one you want

As I passed the time in my uninspiring cubicle that summer, I invested more and more mental energy wondering how things would work out between me and Tess. Honestly, it's kind of embarrassing to talk about – it wasn't exactly healthy. But it was all I could manage at the time. The connection we made before she left was palpable. That, combined with a boring project and little else going on in my personal life, overwhelmed me – hook, line, and sinker.

I didn't realize at the time just how dangerous this kind of thinking was. When we invest this much energy on one specific thing, we subconsciously tell our brains that thing is of life-or-death importance. When our brains identify anything as being extraordinarily important, they come to view said thing as a potential source of both great pleasure and great pain.

In the case of developing feelings for someone, our brains see both the joy of ending up with that person and the despair of things not working out as possible outcomes. Even though we'd prefer to focus on the former, we sometimes find we can't. Our brains see the despair as a threat to our well-being and hijack our mental capacities. They put us on the defensive in order to move us away from the distress as soon as possible.

As we've seen before, this kind of defense was paramount when we were outrunning predators in the wild. But when we're sitting in our cubicles or out on a date? Not so much. Without consciously dialing back this hyperfocus on our fears, we run the risk of burning out or running right into them.

DRIVING INTO THE WALL

Going on the defensive to avoid painful outcomes mirrors an interesting concept from race car driving, oddly enough, and contains the same potential pitfalls of which we should be aware. The logic is that when you lose control of your car and start to spin out, the area of the track you focus on determines where your car will ultimately end up.

One of the scariest destinations for drivers is the wall. Slamming into it typically means substantial damage to their vehicles and bodies. In an attempt to avoid the wall during a spinout, most drivers stare right at it. They think keeping their eyes on it will help them navigate away from it. However, drivers who employ this strategy actually hit the wall far more often than those that do not.

Though it may seem unrelated, we can apply this same lesson to our understanding of anxiety. When we obsess over an outcome we want from a fear-inducing situation, we make the other potential outcomes in the situation look like the walls of the race track. Then, in an attempt to move away from those negative outcomes, we often get laser-focused on them and drive straight into them.

In order to not drive into the wall, so to speak, we must first take a step back and evaluate the potential outcomes of the situation or idea that's scaring us. Often, though of course not always, when we do so, we realize our minds have made our walls seem much bigger than they really are. When I found myself at my client's office, fretting over what would happen between me and Tess, I employed this same strategy.

Through brainstorming, I realized so many different outcomes were possible from the situation. She could come back and we could start dating. She could also come back and I could decide she wasn't right for me. After all, we had only been out twice previously. She could also return and realize I wasn't right for her. Though I knew this last outcome would be pretty challenging (my "wall"), I also knew, deep down, it couldn't be much worse than what I was putting myself through at that very moment.

Sure, it would be extremely disappointing, but somehow I'd get through it. Just being able to make that distinction signaled to my brain that the wall wasn't so big anymore, which cooled my anxiety a bit. Of course, I was still looking straight at that wall, but now, I was wearing slightly more protective padding to cushion the blow. In time, maybe I'd even be able to look over at the infield.

Only in truly evaluating our potential outcomes and what they mean can we put things in perspective and see the true size of our walls. When our anxious minds are moving at breakneck speed, we often forget to take a step back and get that perspective. This causes our walls to appear even larger and more dangerous than they really are.

When you find yourself in the depths of your own fear, I implore you to leverage this strategy. Ask yourself what could result from the situation you're turning over in your mind, then ponder what each result would truly mean to you. Once you have those meanings, I'll bet you find it slightly easier to pump the breaks, look at a more desirable outcome, and start moving in that direction.

LOOKING AT THE INFIELD

When we focus on not driving into our walls, we usually forget that our car could very well end up somewhere else on the track, unscathed. While Tess was out of the country, I was so worried about what would happen between us that I lost sight of what I actually wanted – her to be my girlfriend.

In my moment of clarity that summer, I realized this blunder, and muttered to myself, "Holy shit, man, you're so afraid of freaking out and messing things up that you're forgetting there's a decent chance you'll be the happiest person on earth when she comes back. Why not just try to think about that and let the rest work itself out?"

That was the moment in which I finally reconnected to what I actually wanted out of the situation. And, man, did it feel better. Without remembering what it is you're truly after, putting yourself through anxiety sometimes makes you feel like you're suffering for no reason. Connecting back to what you actually want out of the situation can put things in a positive perspective.

Now, before we dive into the details of this tactic, I need to make you aware of one of its inherent risks – getting back in your head over the outcome you want. This happens, or can happen, when you unintentionally use the strategy to re-enter patterns of looping-thinking. That is, you don't actually *reconnect* to your desired end but instead worry about it again. Thus, when leveraging this step, it's important to remember to not get caught up in the details. Simply remember the outcome you want quickly, and see if it makes you feel any better.

When we quickly reconnect to what we want out of an anxious situation, we can *turn our fears around.* So often we look at only the negative potential outcomes of a situation and neglect the really good ones. If we don't take a minute to stop and get our brains off autopilot, we run the risk of never reconnecting to the goal or outcome we're after.

This practice can be applied to most of the situations that evoke our greatest fears. For example, let's say you're giving a speech to a large audience in the coming days. As soon as you think about the task, you worry about what could go wrong in the situation. You conjure up thoughts of peeing your pants on stage, fainting, or forgetting your lines.

These aren't the only possibilities from the situation, they're just the ones our defensive brains tend to come up with in threat-detection mode. When we take a moment to breathe and slow down our thoughts surrounding the situation, we often find we can more easily connect to the positive potential outcomes in play.

For example, maybe you agreed to give the speech because you'll be talking about a cause near and dear to your heart. Wouldn't it be amazing to have several people come up to you afterward and say your words really resonated with them? Without slowing down your thinking, you may forget these exciting possibilities even exist.

In all anxious situations, there's a positive potential outcome you can get hopeful or excited about. It's just that, sometimes, we infuse such outcomes with so much angst that reminding ourselves of them isn't helpful. When you find yourself in a scenario like this, don't fret. Just go back to breathing deeply and try to put your mind on something else.

Of course, some situations in life make it seem like only negative potential outcomes are in play. For example, if someone in your family is suffering from a life-threatening illness, your fears might make you feel like only the worst-case scenario is possible. However, even under these daunting circumstances, there exists the possibility that your family member will make a full recovery.

In my mind, and it goes without saying that this is way easier said than done, it makes the most sense to remind yourself of the possibility of that recovery. When we do the opposite and project our future fears into the current moment, we lose our presence and diminish our ability to spend cherished time with that family member.

Even though our innate worries often engulf us and sidetrack us from our greatest desires, it's our duty to slow ourselves down and take the blinders off when we're feeling fearful. Only then can we reconnect to the outcomes we want most and safely navigate away from the race track walls of our minds.

STEP FOUR

Shift your focus to something positive

We've discussed the concept that thoughts are things – each thought we think sends an electrical impulse into our bodies, and each impulse carries with it the capacity to influence how we feel, both physically and mentally. It goes without saying then, that what we focus on, we feel inside. When we bombard ourselves with negative and disempowering thoughts, we precipitate our own anxious symptoms.

The longer we focus on one specific thought, the more power we give it. That's why it's so dangerous to get in our heads – negative thoughts gain momentum and make us feel more anxious the longer we stew on them. Thus, in order to mitigate our fears, we must make sure we're only focusing on things that carry us away from our feelings of unrest.

During the summer that Tess was away, I spent a good amount of time each day wondering how things would play out between us. Sure, some part of me was excited about the prospect of us dating upon her return, but I'd placed so much importance on the uncertain outcome that it was very hard for me to think of anything but losing her. There were months between us. She could forget about me, lose interest, or start seeing someone else.

All of those negative outcomes scared the crap out of me and begged for my attention. Undisciplined in my thinking, I gave in to their requests and focused on them intently. As I did this, my anxiety expanded and my fears felt even more real. This wasn't an isolated incident either – this is how anxiety works in general, and is exactly why getting in our heads is so hazardous.

When we aren't disciplined in our thinking and let our fears permeate our minds, we subject ourselves to elevated levels of stress and fear. When we obsess over avoiding something we don't want – be it a panic attack or symptom we commonly associate with anxiety – we only experience more of it.

Recent psychological research explains the reason for this phenomenon: when we think about our fears, our minds can barely tell the difference between our visualizations and the real thing.[19] Our bodies react with all sorts of negative emotions as if we're already experiencing the very situation we're dying to avoid.[20]

In order to prevent our negative feelings and anxiety from propagating, we must be vigilant about keeping our focus off our fears. Just because something feels threatening doesn't mean we always need to focus on it. We've evolved quite a bit since our days of living in caves and outrunning predators. In situations devoid of true danger, it's imperative you try to keep your focus on something that excites you or, at the very least, doesn't make you feel like total shit any time you think about it.

RECURSIVELY ANXIOUS

Controlling our focus is not as easy as most people would lead us to believe. It's actually pretty difficult, especially once our thoughts pick up steam. We often become so wrapped up in fretting about our fears that we don't even realize what we're doing – making ourselves miserable with misguided, negative thinking. One of the reasons it can be so difficult to control our focus is that we often beat ourselves up for not being able to switch from a set of scary thoughts to a set of empowering ones. Here's an example.

---

[19] Waugh, Christian, et al. "Cardiovascular and Affective Recovery from Anticipatory Threat." *Biological Psychology*, vol. 84, no. 2, May 2010, pp. 169–175., doi:10.1016/j.biopsycho.2010.01.010.
[20] Restak, Richard. "How Our Brain Constructs Our Mental World." *The Naked Brain*, Three Rivers Press, 2006, pp. 62-63.

Let's say you have to give an important sales pitch next week. You know this pitch will determine whether or not you'll make quota for the quarter. As you think about this presentation, the magnitude of the situation takes over, and within seconds, you feel terribly anxious about the whole thing.

Soon, the prospect of *not* landing the deal becomes the only thing you can think about. Your inability to focus on actually winning the business kills you inside and makes you feel like a loser. In anger, you lash back at yourself, screaming, "Why am I so anxious?! Why can't I just focus on this?!" The frustration only builds as you beat yourself up, making yourself even more anxious in the process.

This phenomenon is what I would call *going down the anxiety rabbit hole*. The hole is as deep as however many times you react negatively to being anxious. It could go on forever. First, you might just be anxious. But then, you might get mad at yourself for feeling scared and become anxious over being anxious. Thus, further down the hole you go.

There's a term from computer programming that describes this phenomenon as well, and it's called *recursion*. In computer science, recursion is the process by which a software function calls itself, often repeatedly.[21] In the real world, recursion sometimes occurs when you place two mirrors or webcams so they face one another and look back into each other again and again, creating what appears to be an endless set of repeating images.

When you beat yourself up for being anxious, your anxiety becomes recursive. It calls itself again and again, gaining momentum in the process. As you can imagine, this can be quite harmful. From my experience, there are two hacks that can help get you out of this hole. The first is to stop beating yourself up about being anxious. Put your foot down and say, "I don't care if I'm anxious. It is what it is. I'm done making myself feel worse about it." This giving up

---

[21] Hetland, Magnus Lie. "Counting 101." *Python Algorithms: Mastering Basic Algorithms in the Python Language*, 1st ed., Apress, 2010, p. 56.

of the fight against your fears becomes your escape rope back to the surface.

The second way out of the anxiety rabbit hole is to remember that thinking about the things you want to happen in a given situation is far less important than not thinking about the things you don't want to happen. For most of our lives, our teachers, coaches, and society in general have told us we need to visualize the outcomes we want to achieve; only then can we make them reality.

But this really isn't true. Just think about all the things you do and achieve on a daily basis that you don't think about at all. Take weightlifting, for example. Sure, sometimes you may first visualize yourself bench pressing your way to a new personal record, but sometimes you instead just get up there and do it. Whether you visualize it first doesn't matter all that much. What does matter is you stay out of your head and give yourself an opportunity to perform your best.

The truth is, we live most of our lives on autopilot, and that's not necessarily a bad thing. We come home, talk to our family, and cook dinner without thinking too much about it. We clean the dishes and put the kids to bed without obsessing over those things either. Being able to operate without calculating every move helps our brains and bodies be more efficient, and is actually a pretty good thing.

If we can get ourselves to perform the tasks that make us anxious in the same autopilot-directed way that we clean our dishes, then we'll greet those tasks with far less anxiety than we did previously. I remember how skeptical I was of these very words just a few years ago. I used to overthink everything and feel that if I didn't, what I wanted out of an upcoming situation wouldn't come to fruition. After going through a multitude of these situations and coming out on the other side of many of them with the outcomes I desired, I realized this kind of obsessive thinking isn't necessary.

Of course, that's not to say visualization can't be helpful. It's just that, as I mentioned in the introduction of this book, once fear infiltrates our visions of what we want, it can be very difficult to think about our desires without making ourselves feel anxious. Worse yet, once we're anxious about not being able to envision our desired outcomes, we often beat ourselves up and fall down the rabbit hole.

As with all strategies, one may work for one person while it doesn't for someone else. The key to this one is to visualize only when you find it uplifting, and not beat yourself up when you are unable to do so. To do anything else, in my mind, would be self-sabotage.

FOCUS ON WHAT YOU CAN CONTROL

Let's jump back to our hypothetical situation of you preparing for your big sales pitch. So you're anxious about it and all you can think of is the fact that you might not win the client over. This very idea eats you up inside. One day, however, you put your frustration aside. You step back and ask yourself, "Am I really in control of whether this client buys from me?" After a few seconds of thinking, you get your answer – probably not.

Sure, you know the VP of the company you're pitching, but so does one of the sales reps from your largest competitor. As is the case in many important, uncertain situations, the outcome of this pitch is not necessarily under your control – and that's okay. In instances like these, we just need to focus on the things we *can* control, so we can leverage them to *influence* the outcome as best we can.

In this specific scenario, no matter how much you worry about the pitch, you will not change your client's mind or alter their decision. What company they choose to do business with is ultimately up to them. However, how they think about who they should choose is influenced by a variety of factors, one of them being who had the most compelling pitch. Thus, instead of worrying about whether you'll win the contract, you should put your focus on creating the best proposal possible.

So many circumstances in life follow this pattern. We get so focused on an outcome we can't control that we forget there are many factors in the situation we actually do have control over. In the situation with my friend Tess, the same logic applied. When it came down to it, it really wasn't up to me whether she wanted to date me or not. I could not control her decision. However, I did have some influence.

If I never texted her again or just flat out ignored her, she probably wouldn't have wanted to talk to me again. Yet, if I stayed in touch with her, kept our conversations engaging and interesting, and showed I cared, I would certainly leave a good impression on her. Again, sometimes outcomes aren't up to us, but that doesn't mean we can't influence them. It's our responsibility to determine what that influence is, focus on it, and put our best foot forward.

STEP FIVE

Recite a powerful mantra

It's pretty clear the role uncertainty plays in anxiety. Thus, it should make sense when I say that in order to quell our fears, we'll either need to lessen the amount of uncertainty surrounding any given anxious situation or become more comfortable with uncertainty in general. In this chapter, we'll focus on the former by talking about mantras.

A mantra, which I would loosely classify as an empowering short sentence or collection of words, is a tool I often employ to drive certainty back into my body during anxiety-riddled situations. The logic is pretty straight forward. Anxious situations entail massive amounts of uncertainty. Uncertainty over how things will turn out, what will happen, how we'll react, and so on. In these situations, what we really need is a way of driving that uncertainty out so we feel better about the situation as a whole.

Mantras are our tool for doing just that. They're a tactic we can leverage to change our state quickly. When we recite uplifting mantras, we actively flood our minds and bodies with certainty, which begins the process of driving out the uncertainty.

All that matters in using a mantra is that it feels powerful to you. By powerful, I mean it should evoke strong, positive emotions within you. Your mantra will be one of your go-to tactics in dark times, after all. You should be confident that any time you use it, you'll be able to evoke those beneficial emotions quickly.

I know the idea of using a mantra to change how you're feeling might seem not believable or even a little bizarre. But the truth is, we use them in our lives all the time, whether we know it or not. For example, on my walk home the other day, I realized I left my computer charger at the office. Annoyed with myself, I kept repeating, "I'm such an idiot! How could I have forgotten my charger?!" Of course, repeating this kind of language to myself didn't make me feel good. But it did change my state as I replayed it over and over in my mind.

When we're frustrated or angry, we frequently use mantras in this fashion. When things don't go our way, we exclaim, "Are you freaking kidding me?!" creating negative energy inside ourselves that often sends us spiraling downward. The good news is we need not always use mantras to make ourselves feel worse. We can also leverage them to get ourselves out of states of panic, fear, or stress. That very idea is what we'll be focusing on in this chapter.

BREATHING. FOCUS. OUTCOME.

One of my favorite mantras is "Breathing. Focus. Outcome." I especially love this mantra because it walks me through a short list of steps I can leverage to feel better almost immediately. First, this mantra tells me to take a look at my breathing. As we talked about in step one, we often stop breathing properly during times of stress. Reciting this mantra reminds me to watch my breath so I can activate my parasympathetic nervous system and get my body out of the fearful state faster.

Next, this mantra tells me to check my focus. I know that what makes me anxious, most often, is focusing on something I don't want to happen. When I recite this mantra, I quickly get to a place of awareness where I can determine whether my focus is helping me feel good or not. If I determine it's not, I come up with something else to focus on and try to leave the old focus behind. Though this is sometimes easier said than done, continuing to recite the mantra helps me hammer a new focus into my mind.

Lastly, this mantra reminds me to revisit what I really want from the anxious situation in front of me. This is important because, as we saw in step three, our fears often consume us and make us lose sight of the outcomes we're truly after. Consciously asking myself what I want out of the scary situation helps me shift my focus back to the desired outcome my fears distracted me from.

Though I did come up with this mantra myself, I'd be delighted if you adopted it for your own practices. The only word of caution I'll give in using it is to not let it stress you out if you have a hard time changing your focus or thinking about your desired outcome. As we covered in the previous chapter, beating yourself up over not being able to control your focus will only make you even more anxious than you already are.

There's nothing wrong with not thinking about your desired outcome if it's causing you stress. When it does, just go back to the first part of the mantra – focus on your breathing and let your parasympathetic nervous system get you back to calm. The sooner you get there, the easier it will be to change your focus anyway.

IF YOU GET IN YOUR HEAD, YOU'RE DEAD

Another one of my favorite mantras comes from the personal development pioneer, Tony Robbins. If you haven't heard of Tony, he's one of the best success coaches in the industry and is well-known for his life-changing seminars and impeccable psychology. He's an absolute force of nature and has helped some of the biggest names on the planet get out of funks and return to prime form. He's one of my personal heroes and has made a massive impact on my life.

I've adopted one of Tony's catch phrases as one of my personal mantras. That mantra states, "If you get in your head, you're dead." It's one of my favorites because it aligns so well with all of my other strategies. It quickly reminds me, when I'm fearful, that overanalyzing things is a metaphorical death sentence.

Of course, just reciting a phrase might not always get us out of our heads. That's why, when I recite this mantra, I often combine it with another powerful strategy that

Robbins advocates. Now I know this is going to sound a bit crazy, but please just hear me out.

When I get nervous, anxious, or in my head, I like to stand up tall and make fists with both of my hands. Then, I start pounding my chest with both fists at the same time. I keep pounding about once a second while simultaneously saying to myself, "If you get in your head, you're dead." If I'm at my house, I'll scream this tagline. If I'm at work or in public, I might just whisper it instead. The volume of the incantation is not nearly as important as the physical act itself.

Again, I know it probably sounds bizarre, but there's a method to the madness. When we employ this strategy in an anxious situation, we take all the uncertain energy surrounding the situation and use it to drive certainty back into our bodies. By engaging our entire bodies with such energy and conviction, we literally push that uncertainty out. Moreover, we give our minds something new to focus on. Repeat this action often enough leading up to an anxiety-provoking situation, and you'll be well on your way to getting out of your head.

So, how can this chest-pounding behavior be applied to a specific situation like going to a rock climbing gym for the first time? I'm glad you asked. When I go climbing or perform any other task that scares me, I engage in this behavior before the task, then continue to repeat, "If you get in your head, you're dead" to myself throughout the scary activity. Both before and during rock climbing, repeating this phrase gives me something to focus on other than what could go wrong. Most often, it's that scary possibility that becomes the catalyst for getting into our heads. If we stay focused, we can increase the likelihood of an anxiety-free climb.

The two mantras I described here are just a couple I use in my battle. They may or may not work for you, so feel free to use them or come up with one of your own. If you opt for the latter approach, just make sure your mantra is short, memorable, and empowering. Don't worry about it being the *right* one. There is no right or wrong mantra. There's only the mantra that feels good to *you*.

STEP SIX

Stop questioning yourself

Most of the times we're feeling fearful, we're questioning a belief we hold. We all hold many beliefs, including those about ourselves, the world, or how we think certain events might unfold. When we question our beliefs, we build more uncertainty around them and make ourselves feel stressed out and anxious.

The act of questioning is an important one in our lives, albeit in the right places. When we're trying to disprove a theory in science class, questioning is what helps us get to our answer. But when we're contemplating our ability to achieve a goal, questioning breeds self-doubt and sends us back down the rabbit hole.

The reason why questioning our abilities or how something will play out is so dangerous is that when we start to question anything, we automatically begin to believe the very thing we're questioning, less. When we believe something less, we feel more uncertainty over that very thing, which only increases the likelihood that we'll get stuck in our heads and feel even more anxious about it.

Take this situation for example. As part of your job at a local accounting firm, you're required to scan and upload hundreds of tax returns a day to your company's online storage system. This started out as just a small portion of your job, but you showed such speed and reliability with the task early on that your company appointed you as the go-to person for doing this. As such, both you and your boss are confident in your ability to get the job done quickly and accurately.

One day, however, you get a bit distracted while scanning some of the returns, and a few of them fall on the ground. You pick them back up and scan them as planned, not realizing that as they hit the ground, they shuffled together, resulting in many of them containing pages from other documents.

A few days later, your boss goes to retrieve several files from the online portal and notices they're all messed up – some of them have too many pages, and others, too few. He runs to your desk and, out of frustration, blurts out, "How could you let this happen? Our clients' returns are vital to the success of our business! We shredded the original documents – we're screwed!"

Rattled, you ask yourself how you could have been so careless. Your boss trusted you, and you let him down. That does not sit well with you. Soon, the thoughts and questions come faster. "How the heck did I mess those files up? What if I've been mixing documents up this whole time?" These questions don't lead to answers, only more questions and anxiety. You leave work a little late that night, after trying to do some damage control, seriously contemplating whether you're any good at your job.

Though it's a simple, fictitious story, it highlights how we often engage in similar unproductive mental exercises in the heat of anxious situations. We dive deeper into the uncertainty of what will come to be, hoping that by questioning how we believe the situation will play out, we'll feel better and more secure about it. This is not how anxiety works, however. Anxiety feeds off our questions and doubts. No matter how difficult it may be, we must refuse to question ourselves in anxiety-provoking situations if we want to evade our fears.

For example, if you have a doctor's appointment coming up and are scared about the bill of health you'll receive, first remind yourself of what you want (a clean bill of health), then resolve to fend off questions surrounding the belief that you'll get it. Don't project yourself in the situation, and don't try to imagine how everything will occur. Just show up to the appointment as you would any other normal event in your life, and you'll likely find that your anxiety over it subsides quicker than usual.

The same logic can be applied to any frightening situation. Our freak outs don't just come from nowhere – we bring them about as we question our beliefs surrounding the outcome of the situation. I've found that if you drop the questioning, you not only lessen the anxiety, but you also simultaneously reconnect to and strengthen the beliefs you've been calling into question the whole time.

STOP WORRYING ABOUT THE HOW

Previously, I described the anguish I put myself through when preparing for my first skydive. During those fearful days, I tried to picture myself, first, at the edge of the plane, then, amongst the clouds, wind rushing through my hair. The only problem was, no matter how hard I tried, all I could visualize was what could go wrong on my skydive. This not only scared me – it also really frustrated me. I fought back against these visualization shortcomings and made myself feel worse as I burned all my mental energy.

Fighting back against anxiety and frustration is just another way of going further and further down the rabbit hole. The deeper you go, the harder it is to get out. At the time, I didn't realize this. I'd always heard that successful people use visualization in the process of achieving their goals. I thought I was just doing what they were doing. It turns out I was not.

What I was actually doing was dwelling on my fears and obsessing over the minute details of the jump. Though I began with the intention of truly visualizing a successful skydive, things took a quick, but subtle, turn from there. I went from picturing myself doing something exciting to trying to reason my way out of experiencing something I didn't want, without even realizing it. This is, case in point, why visualization in the face of anxiety is so treacherous.

On a subconscious level, our minds know we can't possibly predict how a situation will come to be. They see our incessant questioning of how a scary event will play out not as an honest attempt to gain clarity, but as a sign something is wrong. In turn, they sound the anxiety alarms.

There's absolutely nothing wrong with not being able to visualize the outcome you desire, nor is that required in order to achieve said outcome. So many of us get ourselves caught up in these crazy thought patterns and incessantly try to push through them in order to conjure up the outcome we want from an anxious situation. This is insanity.

Visualization is supposed to feel good. It's meant to be centered around something positive – be it achieving one of your goals or fantasizing about something you'd love to happen one day. It's not supposed to be focused on something you want to avoid, nor is it meant to be time-consuming or stressful.

If you're worrying about the *how*, you're probably experiencing the innate difficulty of visualizing something you want once it's become wrapped up with your fears. When you find yourself doing this, remember that you don't need to envision what you want in order to achieve it. Just take the stress as a sign to move on, and stop beating yourself up. You'll thank me later.

WE'RE WORSE AT PREDICTING THAN WE THINK

I have a story that I think will drive these concepts home for good. Last year, I was talking with my friend Frank. He told me he'd been spending quite a bit of time wondering how he would eventually meet a special girl and make her his girlfriend. He's a bit of an anxious person, so just like me, he tends to get in his head about things that are important to him. He really wanted to be in a relationship and was starting to lose hope that he'd find one.

Most days, he mentioned, he'd sit at his desk at work, picturing himself out at stores and restaurants, striking up conversation with various women. He'd go into such detail in his visualizations, picturing everything from what he was wearing, to what he was saying, to what music was playing. He often spent so much time obsessing over every last detail that he wore himself out. He really did think these tactics

64

would help, but they didn't. Yet still, he had a hard time giving them up. He figured if he could just push through and visualize the exact situation in which he'd meet his girlfriend, he'd finally be able to stop obsessing.

Months went by, and with our busy schedules, Frank and I didn't keep in touch as much as we would've liked to. One day, however, he called me. He was practically screaming into the phone with excitement. "Dude, you wouldn't believe what happened last night! I was just standing around at the bar with my friend, when all of a sudden, this stunning woman turned the corner and walked right up to me. We talked for hours and exchanged numbers! We're going out this week! I have absolutely no idea how it happened! It was amazing!"

I was so happy for Frank. It was obvious this whole subject had been eating him up inside, and it seemed as though his world had just been turned upside down, in a good way, overnight. As I hung up the phone that day, I couldn't help but think: we have just about no idea how *anything* is going to play out in our lives. Sure, we might know we're going to a baseball game tomorrow night, but we could never predict that we'd randomly sit next to an old friend from high school or spill beer all over ourselves. The same was true with Frank. No matter how much he tried to predict how he'd meet his girlfriend, none of that preparation actually mattered when it came to the real thing.

We are not meant to predict our entire lives, nor are we meant to live them in our heads. Sure, some things require our analytical capacities like doing our taxes or figuring out whether a stock is worth investing in. But many things do not. Life really is meant to be lived from the heart and in the moment. When we're at the bar or flying through the sky with a parachute strapped to our backs, there's no time to be analytical. There's only time to drink in what's going on around us. These moments should teach us something – no matter how far we get into our heads prior to them, there's no more effective, nor rewarding, strategy than letting our hearts do the talking when we find ourselves in said situations.

STEP SIX

When you're freaking out about how an upcoming, important situation will play out, ask yourself if you're stuck in your head or actually operating from your heart. If the answer is the former, remind yourself it's not your responsibility to figure out *how* things will play out. Then, reconnect to *what* you want out of the situation, trust that you'll know what action to take to make that outcome yours when you're in the situation, and let the chips fall where they may.

STEP SEVEN

Utilize an empowering way to feel good, right now

We Americans love our vices. Soda, candy, desserts, alcohol, cigarettes – you name it. With our overindulgences, we've become one of the most unhealthy, overweight countries in the world. I'm a firm believer that a release from time to time can help you keep your sanity. However, when we abuse these vices, we can get ourselves into big trouble. So, why do we continue to misuse them despite knowing they don't serve us over the long term? For many of us, it's because we often find ourselves stressed out and uninspired and these powerful distractors help us feel good at a moment's notice.

Vices such as candy, cigarettes, and alcohol can have a profound impact on our mental state and physiology. They can give us a little boost when we're feeling down, frustrated, or bored. Yet, just because they help us escape reality momentarily, that doesn't mean we should always be so quick to reach for them. When we constantly rely on such vices for our well-being, or at least our temporary highs, we diminish our power to make ourselves feel good – the very thing we're after when we're feeling anxious. The more we diminish our influence over how we feel, the less frequently we remember we can make ourselves feel good just about anytime we choose.

I don't think any of this should come as a surprise – we've talked about the impact our thoughts have on our mental state quite a bit throughout this book so far. In this chapter, I'd like to continue that discussion by introducing two new empowering ways we can get ourselves out of fearful mental states on demand.

The first method I'd like to discuss is the recall of a powerful, pleasant memory. Now I know this might come off as a bit sappy, but it has worked for me, so I'd recommend giving it a try yourself. When I'm feeling really anxious, I often think back to a particularly exciting memory of mine that evokes positive emotion and gets me out of my head.

One memory I think of is the day I received my acceptance letter to Boston College. Throughout high school, I was obsessed with getting into BC. It was the perfect fit for me – a prestigious university close to home with great academics and a Division I sports program. I wanted it so bad I could taste it.

For the previous three years, I dedicated everything I did in the classroom and on the field to getting into my dream school. I saw every good grade or successful track meet as a way to boost my standing. I studied for hours every night and retook my standardized tests several times to make sure I gave myself the best shot. I wouldn't let anything stop me from getting accepted.

On a Saturday morning in mid-December of my senior year, my friend Isaac instant messaged me. He said BC decisions were coming in the mail that day. He had just gotten his. This was the day I was waiting for. I was so excited and so nervous. I watched out the window for what seemed like hours, waiting for the mailman to come. When I finally heard the mail truck's engine bumbling up the street toward my house, my heart raced. I watched the mailman walk down our driveway with the mail, then head back toward his truck. I sprinted out to the mailbox, dressed in my BC apparel. I had no idea what the decision would be.

I stuck my hand in the mailbox and closed my eyes. I could barely stand to open them. When I finally did, I saw a large envelope staring right back at me. It was at that moment I knew I'd gotten into my dream school. Beyond excited, I ran back into my house and, judging by the look on my face, my parents knew what had come in the mail. We spent the next couple of hours celebrating. It was one of the happiest days of my life, and every time I think about it, I can't help but smile and be thankful.

Now I tell you that story not to brag, but to show you the power of a happy memory. When you're in the middle of an anxious situation and put all of your focus on a specific, happy memory, that memory often pushes what's troubling you out of your mind, even if only temporarily. Such recollections are so powerful because they serve as easy, effective ways to change your focus and feel good. Since these memories have already occurred, we can return to them whenever we choose, without feeling uncertain or anxious.

The second way to make yourself feel better at a moment's notice is to create a compelling vision for your future and think about that vision whenever you're feeling fearful. When you come up with a vision of what you want your future to look like, it should pull you forward and help guide you. For example, I have a vision of publishing this book and using it to help people suffering from anxiety make massive strides in their battles with mental health. That vision fires me up and makes me feel good. It also guides me in my actions. I know I need to finish this book, publish it, and then market it in order to make the vision come to life.

What would you like to see come true in your future? Would you like to run your own business? Travel the world? Move to a paradise island? I don't care how far-fetched it seems to you. Just think about whatever excites you and make that your vision. Then, when you're feeling down or anxious, return to that vision and use it to pick yourself back up. When you think about obtaining that vision, you should see your fears diminish, even if only temporarily.

Keep both your positive past memories and visions for your future in your back pocket and pull them out when you're stuck in your head. They're some of your go-tos for feeling better immediately. As you start to use them more and more, you may even find that these tools perk you up more than candy or soda ever could. And good news – both of them come without the sugar crash.

STEP EIGHT

Get back to the present moment

A few years ago, on a Sunday in September, with Tess still on her extended vacation, I headed to my parents' house to watch football as I often do during the NFL season. It had been a long week, and I was sufficiently wrapped up in my head, worrying again about whether things would work out between us.

By the time I got to my parents' house that day, I was so out of it I could barely hold a conversation. My thoughts were negative and unrelenting. My mother and father tried countless times to strike up conversation with me. I answered all of their questions as quickly as possible so I could get back in my head. It felt awful, but was all I could manage at the time.

My family and I didn't have much meaningful dialogue that day. I didn't engage and open up enough to allow it. No one said anything to me about acting distant, but as I left the house that night, I was completely embarrassed. I usually felt great on these Sundays, after taking in a meaningful day spent with family. But that night was different. That night, I was regretful.

I *hadn't* taken in a meaningful day with my family. Instead, I'd shut myself off from that possibility. I'd wasted a great opportunity to connect with my parents, brother, and sister-in-law. I'd been at my parents' house physically, but not mentally. My mind was in Europe, with Tess. I'd tried to fight against a still unforeseen outcome, and, despite all my efforts, still didn't feel any better. If I had to succinctly explain why I felt the way I did that day, I'd say it was because *I wasn't present.*

Anxiety emerges when we try to live in moments outside of the one in front of us. All we have is the present moment. Nothing else is guaranteed to us. Our brains know this, on some level, and sound the alarms when they realize we're living, mentally, somewhere in the future.

Unfortunately, future-oriented thinking can be hard to break out of. That's because worrying about what will happen next week or a year from now often causes us to overlook the things in front of us that could make us feel a sense of joy immediately. Sure, it's difficult to always live in the moment, but if we did, we'd probably feel better more often and struggle with our fears far less frequently.

The concept that anxiety can't get to us when we're fully immersed in the present moment is one of the main ideas in Eckhart Tolle's bestselling book, *The Power of Now*. In his work, Tolle states that just about all of our pains in life come from living outside of the here and now.[22] When we focus our minds on all the wonderful things currently going on around us, we give ourselves the best shot at finding peace and happiness, Tolle says.

STRATEGIES FOR FINDING PRESENCE

If we're going to be effective at pulling ourselves out of acute, anxious situations, we need to figure out ways to get back to the present moment regardless of difficulty. I suggest three methods for doing so:

1. Practice gratitude
2. Take a moment to observe the world around you
3. Engage in an activity that puts you in flow

When it comes to gratitude, all we have to do is stop once in a while and consciously give thanks for some of the amazing things in our lives. You might be grateful for your

---

[22] Tolle, Eckhart. "Consciousness: The Way out of Pain." *The Power of Now: A Guide to Spiritual Enlightenment*, Namaste Publishing, 2004, p. 33.

family, your dog, or your job. Whatever it is, stop and just say *thank you* for that very thing.

When you engage in gratitude practices, you slow down your observance of time. You take your focus off the countless things you need to do today or the big events on the horizon that scare you. This shift in focus pulls you back into the present moment. It's hard to be afraid of what's coming up next week when you're thinking about, and appreciating, what you have here today.

The same goes for taking a moment to observe the world around you. When you stop to marvel at the colorful flowers in a garden on your walk to work, you launch yourself into the here and now, a place where your fears can't immediately access you. The reason this is so important is that there's almost always something captivating in front of you that you can focus on in order to untether from your fears. Many of these beautiful things we overlook when we're stressfully running from one place to the next.

Though certainly not the only other way to get back to the present moment, the last one I want to talk about is engaging in activities that often put you in a *flow state*. A flow state, as described by psychologist Mihaly Csikszentmihalyi, is a state of full immersion and concentration, brought on by an engaging and slightly challenging task.[23] In flow, the rest of the world seems to melt around you, if only momentarily. Your focus narrows to the very thing you're doing and the task itself becomes the end, not just a means to it.

For example, I love shooting around on the basketball court. It's easy for me to enter a flow state when I throw some headphones in and start hitting shots. As I enter my "zone," the whole world seems to melt away, and my focus zeros in on the basket. In flow, we're fully connected to the present moment, far from our anxieties.

There are a million different activities you could engage in to reach flow. I love cooking new recipes, listening

---

[23] Csikszentmihalyi, Mihaly. *Flow: The Psychology of Optimal Experience*, 1st ed., Harper Perennial Modern Classics, 2008, pp. 39–41, 72-77.

to music, working out, snowboarding, and thrill-seeking. When I'm strapped into a roller coaster, speeding at eighty miles per hour, I'm happy as a clam. When the wind is blowing through my hair and my adrenaline is pumping, it's just about impossible for me to think about anything outside of that coaster ride.

I'm sure you'll find that the things that put you in flow vary from mine. The key is to find activities that can be rewarding in and of themselves – ones that are fun to begin with, offer a slight sense of challenge, and provide you with immediate feedback. As you discover the activities that put you in flow most often, incorporate them into your daily routine. Hit a yoga class or go for a bike ride to kick-start a return to calm as soon as the anxiety starts pouring over you.

If you're looking for even more strategies, revisit the steps we've already covered and think about how you could use them to find presence in your own life. For example, maybe a deep breathing exercise could help slow you down and bring you back to the here and now. Or, maybe reciting a new mantra could help you achieve the same thing. One of my favorites for finding presence is, "Be. Here. Now."

STEP NINE

Remind yourself the worst part of anxiety is the waiting

It was a Thursday night during my junior year of college. My roommates were out at the bar, and I was at home. I had an interview the next morning for a summer internship and couldn't afford to be unprepared or hungover for it. I'd been waiting for this interview for weeks and was pretty nervous about it. In an attempt to make myself feel better, I tried countering my anxious energy with positive visualization – or so I thought.

In reality, I did what I'd done several other times that week – I ruminated over how the interview would go, what I'd say the whole time, and whether or not I'd have a panic attack in the office. Despite my attempts to push through these scary thoughts, I only made myself feel worse. Burned out, I eventually went to bed, hoping a restorative sleep would make me feel better about the whole situation.

That next morning, I rolled out of bed late, still feeling anxious about the interview. I showered quickly, threw on a suit, and headed for the train. I was fairly nervous the entire ride. My mind was not on that train, but in the company's office. I tried to make my last mental preparations before stepping into the situation I had been fearing for weeks. When I arrived at the company's office, an assistant greeted me and led me into a room to wait for my interviewer.

Minutes later, my interviewer, John, arrived and we spent the next hour talking business and technology. It seemed like we'd only been chatting for a few minutes, but, just like that, it was over. I felt great. On the way out, I realized just how futile my mental preparations had been. All the fear I'd built over the previous weeks dissipated as soon as the interview began. It was an eye-opening day for me. Though I didn't ultimately get that job, I did draw some key insights from the situation. In my mind, those were more valuable than an offer.

The most important conclusion I drew from the interview was that the worst part of an anxiety-provoking event is not usually the event itself, but the time leading up to it. This is the case in 99% of upcoming situations that scare us. This occurs because, ahead of anxiety-riddled events, our brains crave certainty. They long to know exactly how things will go. As such, they sound the anxiety alarms and push us to rethink every last detail about the event. As we've seen, this is rarely helpful.

When we engage in this type of thinking, we forget that by fighting back against the thought of being anxious tomorrow, we literally change our neurochemistry on the spot. By mentally plotting ways to avoid a panic attack in the future, we just about give ourselves a panic attack *right now*.

Whenever the time between the current moment and an upcoming stressful situation increases, so does the potential for anxiety. More time means more opportunities to obsess over the situation and fall deep down the rabbit hole. To counter the harmful potential of lead time, we must be patient. We must remember that if we want to avoid our fears both today and in that upcoming situation, we must stay out of our heads.

Most often, when that event finally does come to pass, I find it's nowhere near as intense as I've made it out to be in my mind. Even if it does end up being terrible, it's *still* usually not as bad as the despair I've put myself through mentally, leading up to it. As the saying goes, "I've been through some terrible things in my life, some of which actually happened."[24]

Now of course, that's not to say in-the-moment anxiety never happens. It would be naive of me and an oversight to say so. Fearing it is one of the very reasons we get in our heads in the first place. All I mean when I say *the*

---

[24] Origin unknown, often attributed to Mark Twain

worst part of anxiety is the waiting is that the time leading up to an anxious situation is typically worse than the event itself. I don't mean the event is always a breeze.

That leads me into one small wrinkle with this rule that I think is helpful for in-the-moment fear. When we're really dreading an event, sometimes our negative feelings spill over into the situation itself. When they do, we often find our fight-or-flight systems on overdrive during it.

In order to get this system to power down during such situations, we need to let our bodies suss out their surroundings long enough to realize they're safe. Then, our parasympathetic nervous system will kick in and bring us back to calm. Thus, when I say there's a wrinkle in this rule, what I mean is, sometimes the worst part of anxiety is waiting for our PSNS to activate and restore our tranquility.

This waiting can be scary and frustrating, no doubt. Yet, if we just proceed as normal, without resisting our fight-or-flight mechanisms, they'll turn off in just a few minutes. Once that happens, we'll likely lose ourselves in the moment unfolding in front of us, oblivious to the fact that, just a few minutes prior, we were trying to crawl out from the depths of our minds.

THE ANXIETY FACADE

There's one more concept I want to discuss in regard to waiting for an anxiety-provoking event to arrive, and it's what I call *the anxiety facade*. Though it's a bit of a nuance, and doesn't pertain to all anxious situations, it's something I find myself wrestling with quite often. As such, I'd feel irresponsible if I didn't cover it. After discussing this concept, I think you'll be better equipped to identify and manage instances of it in your own life.

The anxiety facade is the outward, gripping appearance our fears present to us in advance of upcoming, uncertain situations. Now, I know what you're probably thinking – that's indicative of almost all anxious scenarios – and you're right. What separates instances involving the facade from all the others, then, is the misdirecting and transient nature of the fear. I'll explain.

Let's pretend you're a budding chef and are about to compete on a live cooking show. Winning this competition would mean everything to you and help pay for the new restaurant you want to open. You know one of the judges on the show, Mike, personally, and remember his favorite food: margherita pizza, your signature dish. All you have to do, you wager, is fire up that pizza, then ride off into the sunset.

In the days leading up to your big appearance, however, you spend a lot of time focusing on what could go wrong on the show. You worry about having a meltdown on set, accidentally cutting yourself with your knife, or dropping your food on the ground. These scary possibilities grip you and make it difficult to focus on anything else.

When you finally get to the competition, you realize you're not nearly as nervous as you had anticipated. You cook a couple tasty pasta dishes for the judges, but come up just short of the prize. As the judges explain their decision, your pal Mike turns to you and says, "You're a pizza guy! I wish you just cooked me a margherita! Then you would've been walking out that door with the money!"

At that moment it hits you: you were so focused on not making a fool out of yourself on national television that you forgot your strategy. Your fears directed you away from your signature dish – the one that likely would've won you the competition. All you're left with is what the frightening facade had been concealing the whole time – regret and disappointment. "Why did I get so nervous? I'm a great chef! I had nothing to worry about!" you exclaim.

This is the epitome of the anxiety facade. In advance of situations where we feel we probably shouldn't be worried, it presents itself and instills great fear in us, then disappears at the last minute. However, even after it's gone, its effects remain. That is, it first distracts us from our desired outcome when we're in the situation we've been fearing, then leaves us disappointed when we vacate said situation without that outcome. This feeling of disappointment is the ugly reality the facade conceals with its daunting appearance. If this isn't all totally clear yet, not to worry. I've got another story from my college days that I think will illustrate this concept even better.

It was junior year, just a few months after I sat for the interview I described earlier in this chapter. I'd hung out with one girl, Sue, quite a bit during first semester, but, to my dismay, she went to Australia to study abroad for the rest of the school year. We said our goodbyes knowing things weren't serious enough to sustain through the long distance, but kept in touch throughout that semester.

When summer finally arrived and she came home, she invited me to her birthday party. I was really nervous. I hadn't seen her in months. In the days leading up to the party, I questioned how it would go, which only made me feel worse about the whole situation.

Despite all the anticipation, on the day of the party, I found I was only slightly anxious. That was the good news. The bad news was I wasn't focused on re-establishing my connection with Sue that night and there were a ton of people at the party. So many, in fact, that I barely got a chance to talk to her; everyone was eager to catch up with the birthday girl. I spent the night chatting with classmates while occasionally looking her way to see if the swarms around her had lessened. They hadn't.

Eventually, I left the party and went to bed disappointed. I'd spent all week preparing for a battle with a panic attack that never came. I woke up the next day feeling like I'd put myself through all of that anguish for nothing. I would've willingly suffered through that anxiety if I'd made some progress toward reviving things with Sue. All I managed was a two-minute conversation with her. It felt like such a waste.

In retrospect, I was so focused on avoiding anxiety and panic at the party that I got distracted from my end goal – rekindling my connection with Sue. Sure, there were lots of other people at that party and they all wanted to talk to her, too. But if I'd made rekindling my main focus rather than avoiding panic, my outlook and strategy likely would've been different. Instead of seeing all the people in attendance and thinking, "Wow, this is daunting," I probably would've thought, "Sure, there are plenty of people here, but I know what I'm after. I'm going to stay focused and give it a fair shot."

I wasn't able to do that and I paid the price for it in disappointment. When we find ourselves struck by this disappointment, we have a choice. We can choose to use it as resolve. We can turn it into motivation for staying out of our heads and ignoring the facade in the days leading up to the events that evoke the most anxiety within us.

If we're able to do so, then we may also be able to retain our focus on the very things we want out of the situation. Even if all we can do is distract ourselves from our anxiety, at the very least, we'll feel better about the situation both leading up to and during it. And that, if nothing else, is a recipe for a better outcome than the one that lies behind the facade.

STEP TEN

Remember this too shall pass

I have a confession to make. This tenth step wasn't part of the original *Ten Steps to Getting Out of Your Head*. Nope, I didn't think of this one until two years after the fateful day at my client's office when I scribed the original list. Even though it didn't make the first draft, it's become an invaluable part of my routine. As such, I felt I had to amend the original framework.

While there are plenty of useful tactics I could always add, I've intentionally capped my list at a memorable ten. *Remember this too shall pass* becomes the finishing touch – the capstone, if you will. It amply ties together several other steps and delivers us a new perspective.

Last summer, the company I worked for got acquired. I didn't think the acquisition was totally negative, so I resolved to see where things went for a while. About five months later, not liking the way things were changing at the company, I decided to look for a new job. I found a posting online that sounded right up my alley and convinced myself I'd be a perfect fit.

I applied for the position and the company got back to me quickly. They wanted me in for an interview! I was stoked. The only problem was I hadn't been on one in three years, and that scared me. The interview wasn't for a week, but that didn't matter – I jumped into my head right then and there. I tried to counteract that jumping by applying the first nine steps in the list. While that helped quite a bit, it didn't get me all the way there. I was missing something, but I didn't know what it was.

After an anxious week, I finally made it to the day of the interview. It was scheduled for the end of the day, so I went to my regular job and tried to power through until then. Shortly after lunch, while sitting at my desk, I realized I was still feeling quite fearful. I decided I needed a quick break, so I headed to the kitchen. I put my water bottle up to the dispenser to fill it. As I watched the water pour in, I thought to myself, "Wow, this has been tough. I've been so anxious all week. I thought I had this figured out. What the hell? When will this end?!"

Just then, one of my coworkers walked into the kitchen and we started talking. We laughed about the pains of a project we both previously worked on, then headed back to our desks. When I got there, I felt good and realized my outlook on the interview wasn't so bad anymore either. "I think I just found the missing piece to the formula," I said to myself.

That insight was the concept that anxiety ebbs and flows; it never stays with us forever and it doesn't stay at the same intensity level for long either. Instead, it rises and falls, regularly. This was evidenced to me by the fact that one minute, I was asking myself, "When will this end?!" and the next, I was thinking my anxiety had taken a short vacation.

Once we realize anxiety rises and falls, we can give ourselves further permission to stop reacting to it when it does rise. We can also give ourselves permission to drop the thoughts and questions that propel our fears, such as "When will this end?!" Think about how powerful this is. If you find yourself in an anxious situation tomorrow that really works you up, instead of freaking out over whether the anxiety will ever subside, you can remind yourself *this too shall pass*.

As your anxiety ebbs and flows, so too will your outlook on the situation you're facing and how you feel about it. I mean just think about it. Let's say you have a big competition coming up next week. Doesn't how you feel, in general, often dictate how you think the competition might go? That is, when you feel good, don't you also feel like the big event is going to go well? Conversely, when you feel like absolute crap before it, doesn't your outlook on the situation go with that feeling? I know it does for me.

The reason I want to emphasize this point is that our attachment to our outlook on a situation influences how long anxiety ultimately sticks with us. Remembering this reminds us not to react so negatively to those outlooks when they're pessimistic, since we know that if we just react less, we can get our anxiety to ebb and our outlooks to turn around faster than they would've otherwise.

Our feelings are constantly changing. The same goes for fear and the symptoms we associate with it – they're all temporary. It's only our thoughts about permanence that sometimes make it feel like our anxiety will never go away. The more we remember that all of these feelings will pass, the less we'll react to them when they do emerge. And the less we react to these negative feelings, the sooner they'll leave us.

Now I'm sure you're wondering just what happened with the job interview from the beginning of this chapter and the anxious situation in general. Well, for starters, I continued leveraging my original steps, as well as this new one, to calm myself down before the interview. Then, I arrived at the company's office with a calmness that helped me perform quite well. So well, in fact, that they made me an offer. And here's the kicker – funny enough, I didn't like that offer, so I turned it down. Yup, the same situation that caused me to worry that they'd laugh me out of the office ended with me holding the cards.

It's funny how life works that way sometimes. It's just another reminder that every negative emotion we experience eventually dissipates. Even during our most anxious times, we must remember that what we're feeling shall pass as well. It's one of the fastest ways to get back to sanity.

PUTTING THE TEN STEPS INTO ACTION

In the opening chapter of this book, I promised I'd present you with a set of tools that would help you manage your anxiety more effectively. As we walked through *The Ten Steps to Getting Out of Your Head*, we covered the first half of those tools – namely, the ones we can apply in the midst of heightened anxious states. Even though I've covered each step in detail already, I want to make sure I really drive these strategies home.

To conclude Part 1 of this book, I'll bring together all the information we covered in the previous ten chapters by applying each step to an everyday, anxiety-provoking situation. As I do that, you'll see how I get myself out of my own head, which, I hope, will inspire you to utilize the steps in your own life. To kick things off, let's revisit *The Ten Steps*:

1. Breathe
2. Determine the true importance of what's making you anxious
3. Evaluate the potential outcomes and reconnect to the one you want
4. Shift your focus to something positive
5. Recite a powerful mantra
6. Stop questioning yourself
7. Utilize an empowering way to feel good, right now
8. Get back to the present moment
9. Remind yourself the worst part of anxiety is the waiting

10. Remember this too shall pass

We've spent a good amount of time talking about women and dates so far, which is a common subject of my anxiety, so I'm going to keep that narrative going by applying *The Ten Steps* to the hypothetical situation of waiting for a first date. Let's jump on in.

It's a Monday night and you have an important date on Friday. Her name is Cindy, and she's a total catch. You saw her at the supermarket last weekend and somehow mustered up the courage to ask her out for drinks. When she accepted your invite, you were on top of the world, fantasizing about falling in love with each other.

Since then, however, you've come crashing back down to reality. The very thought of being out with one of the smartest, prettiest women you've ever dated – yikes. That's a scary thought. You think to yourself, "What happens if it goes poorly? What if I freak out in the middle of it?" The questions you ask yourself send you down a spiral. Feeling out of control, you try to place yourself in the situation. You hope that picturing yourself on the date, not being super nervous, will make things better.

Ten minutes later, you realize this practice hasn't been helpful at all. Your anxiety has taken over and you've fallen down the depths of your mind. Your fear, at this very moment, is palpable. You feel sick to your stomach. "I need to get myself out of this," you tell yourself. "But how?"

In order to get yourself out of your head, you're going to need a strategy. Luckily you have that already, in the form of *The Ten Steps*. Though it might not be easy, what you need to do is walk through all of the steps and apply each one to this situation.

Starting with step one, *breathe*, you begin by inhaling and exhaling slowly and deeply. In doing so, you activate your parasympathetic nervous system, the division of your peripheral nervous system responsible for getting your body back to a resting state. Without breathing fully, it takes longer for this system to engage. Once you start breathing properly, you find yourself more aware of the destructive thought patterns you've been engaging in. This awareness helps you move on to the next step.

While still breathing with purpose, you remember step two. This step reminds you to determine the true importance of what's making you anxious. It also dictates that if you're feeling fearful about something, you're probably making that thing out to be more important than it really is. In thinking about your upcoming date, you remember a couple of the main reasons you're feeling scared. First, Cindy is smart, ambitious, and cute. It's not every day you find that combination. Second, you've had a panic attack while on a date before and that memory alone scares the crap out of you. You never want to experience something like that again.

So you're nervous about screwing up. I know what that feels like, and it certainly isn't fun. But let's think about the bigger picture here. If you blow it with Cindy, are you going to die? It seems doubtful. If you have a panic attack in front of her, is your life over? It may feel like it at the onset of the attack, but, trust me, you'll survive that as well.

One way to really gauge such an event's effect is to think about it in the longer term. Ask yourself, if you have a panic attack in front of Cindy, will it even matter in six months? How about five years? Will you still be saying to yourself down the road, "My whole life was ruined by that panic attack I had in front of that one woman"? Again, it really does seem unlikely. Sure, you might be extremely embarrassed in the moment, but that feeling will most certainly pass with time.

While we're thinking about the future, let's imagine what life could actually be like five years from now. So your date with Cindy was horrendous. You were awkward, you mumbled, and you spilled your first drink. Cindy wasn't as kind as she seemed in the grocery store and actually ended up leaving abruptly. You get upset, but more in a determined, pissed-off kind of way than a helpless one. This determination motivates you to step up your dating game.

You ask out several women that next month and go on quite a few dates. One of those dates, with a woman named Kim, goes extremely well and kick-starts your first long-term relationship. You date for four years, then get engaged. You're so pleased with how things have played out, and you're so excited to build a life with her. As you recall your date with Cindy from several years prior, you think, "Wow, I'm glad that didn't work out because if it did, I never would've met Kim."

Sure, this is all hypothetical reasoning, but the underlying concepts are extremely important. When we put one specific event on a pedestal and make it feel like it's a life or death situation, our brains and bodies respond as though it actually is. Our anxiety flies through the roof and we lose our poise. Making this realization, you feel like you might be sending your brain the wrong message. Hoping to change that, you move on to step number three.

Steps two and three are very similar. The former takes a long-term approach, while the latter focuses more on the immediate potential outcomes of the situation and our attachment to them. As a reminder, step three implores you to evaluate those potential outcomes and reconnect to the one you want. As you examine this step, you realize you've been laser-focused on one of these outcomes specifically – the date going horribly.

As you think about it further, you realize just how destructive this kind of focus has been. You engaged in it all week, and all it did was make you even more apprehensive. You know you don't want to continue to feel this way, so you start looking at all the other potential outcomes from the date. And there are many.

For example, Cindy could be a total snob. She could also think you're a total snob. You could have a little bit of a connection and call it quits after a couple of dates. Or, you could have a strong connection that leads to a relationship with her for a long time. This last one is the one you want. You've just lost sight of it as you've worried about the worst-case scenario occurring. You remind yourself of what it could feel like if this specific result came to fruition. It feels pretty good. With that good feeling, you move on to step four.

The fourth step tells us that, in anxious moments, we must figure out what we're focusing on, and, when necessary, shift that focus to something positive. With your upcoming date, it's obvious what you're obsessing about – not being an anxious mess around Cindy. As a basic rule of thumb: thinking about your fears or your anxiety itself is mental suicide. Don't do it. It's simple and somewhat obvious, but it's amazing how often we overlook this idea. As anxiety veterans, we constantly envision horrible outcomes and worst-case scenarios, despite what we prefer to tell ourselves.

To avoid this pitfall, try putting your focus on something else. Sure, you might not be able to think about this date going well just yet, and there's nothing wrong with that. Instead of beating yourself up about that fact, just shift your focus to something with less anxiety surrounding it.

For example, maybe you have a vacation to Florida coming up next month. Thinking about the vacation will likely make you feel pretty good, even if only for a few minutes. As you change your state through your focus, you start to think that maybe this whole "thoughts are things" idea is pretty spot-on. Sticking with the program, you progress to step number five.

The fifth step tells you to recite a powerful mantra. Though you've been able to calm yourself down slightly with the first four steps, you feel the anxiety starting to build back up. You need something to ground you. You recall a mantra your yoga instructor recited in class the other day. "Everything is going to be alright." You close your eyes and breathe deeply while repeating this mantra to yourself. As you do, you see your focus shift. It feels good to not think about the worst-case scenario for a minute. Soon, you begin to believe the mantra. Trusting this, you move on to step six in the process.

In step number six, we learned that questioning anything you believe in automatically causes you to believe in that very thing, less. As you think back to the beginning of this exercise, you recall the questions that popped into your head as you ruminated over your date with Cindy. Most of these questions were purely negative; wondering what would happen if you freaked out during your date only made you feel worse about the entire thing and brought up even more negative questions in your mind.

With the assistance of this step and some sharp introspection on your part, you realize just how unhelpful your questioning of the date's outcome has been. You remember that when you planned the date, you were super excited. Though you find it difficult (trust me, we all do), you resolve to stop questioning how you think the date will go. Burned out by how much you've analyzed and obsessed over this date, you decide to put your focus on something less polarizing, namely, the rec league basketball game you have tomorrow. Your game last week was one of your best yet. Thinking about it leads us into step seven.

In this step, we said that utilizing empowering ways to feel good immediately is one of the most important things we can do when we're feeling anxious. You could always open the fridge and grab some ice cream or an alcoholic beverage, but those strategies aren't empowering – they're just instant gratification. When looking for empowering methodologies, you should search for either past memories that invigorate you or visions of a compelling future that pull you forward. Remembering the details of this step, you come up with a couple of these visions and use them to move away from the disempowering questions you've been asking yourself in regard to how the date will go.

Closely related to step seven is the very next one in the list – that of the power of presence. In this step, we talked about how, when we're feeling anxious, there's a good chance we're not living in the here and now. Instead, we're likely off in our heads, projecting our fears onto the future.

What we need to do when we find ourselves in this kind of situation is get back into the present moment. Actively seeking to jumpstart this process, you flip back to the three strategies we outlined for regaining presence: practicing gratitude, taking a moment to observe the world around you, and engaging in an activity that puts you in flow.

Knowing you need a strong boost, you opt for the flow route. You think back to the list of flow activities you came up with as you read the chapter on step eight, and decide to pull out your art supplies. There's just something about being in front of a canvas and thinking about what the final product will look like that takes your mind off anything else in your day. But, before you start painting, let's cover the final couple of steps in the list so you can more readily apply all ten the next time you need them.

As you recall step nine, you remind yourself the worst part of anxiety is often waiting for a fear-inducing event to occur. While this step is a bit more passive than the others in the list, it's often one that helps put things in perspective for me. When I'm melting down, I tend to forget the fact that what I'm putting myself through at that very moment is usually as bad as it will ever get.

Making the distinction that the worst part of your date with Cindy is the waiting for it to happen, not the date itself, you signal to your brain that there's far less to be afraid of than you're projecting. Even if things don't go well, you know you'll be able to handle them with grace as you have in disappointing or frightening situations in the past. After all, this is just one date with one woman. With the pressure starting to fall, you feel better than you have throughout this entire process. That positive emotion carries you to the final step in the list.

You made it. Step number ten. In this step, we declared *this too shall pass*. Even in our moments of despair and disappointment, we can find solace in knowing such moments won't last. When we're feeling frightened, it's easy to extrapolate our feelings and draw disempowering, overarching conclusions. For example, "I always get so anxious and feel like crap," or, "My anxiety always crushes me and never lets me go."

These kinds of conclusions are pessimism in action. When we think in this fashion, we forget that nothing in life is constant. Almost everything changes, all the time. The same goes for our anxieties. When you're feeling overwhelmed, remember that feeling is fleeting. Soon, it will change, and so will your outlook on the situation.

Though you lost sight of this knowledge temporarily, re-reading it helps you reconnect with it quickly. Sure, you realize, this situation is nerve-wracking. Your date with

Cindy is important to you. But just because you feel bad right now doesn't mean you'll feel bad forever, nor does it mean the date is destined to go poorly. As you make this distinction, you realize your anxiety will likely ebb and flow throughout the week, and your feelings about how the date will go will likely shift in parallel with it.

Knowing some things are out of your control, you resolve to keep your state in check throughout the week without fighting against the negative feelings that may come your way. Opening yourself up to the fact that things will ebb and flow helps you fight those feelings even less as well. Now having applied all the steps to your anxious situation, you realize you're feeling pretty good. It's at this moment that you decide to grab your canvas and start painting.

So just like that, we took *The Ten Steps* and applied them to an upcoming situation to help get you back toward calm and positivity. Though the situation was theoretical, I don't think it's difficult to see how you could apply this same process to a real situation in your own life.

Since one of the areas in which my anxiety is most active is dating, I thought it would be helpful to show you my approach for mitigating my own fears in regard to that subject. However, *The Ten Steps* are not tied to any specific kind of situation, meaning you can apply them to whatever *you* are going through, be it a scary date or something totally different.

As we now move into the second part of this book, we'll focus less on in-the-moment, acute, anxious situations, and spend more time building upon the foundation we've created already. We'll develop higher-level life practices that will help us avoid getting into as many anxious situations in the first place, and continue to refine what we've discussed thus far. When all is said and done, my hope is you'll be equipped to deal with almost any kind of anxious situation you may face. With that thought, let's continue our journey via part two.

PART 2: ZOOMING OUT

LOOKING FOR THE SOURCES

In the first part of this book, we talked mostly about how we can get ourselves out of anxious states once we've entered them. While such a discussion is paramount to helping us manage our anxiety more effectively, it's just one part of the overall picture. Another major piece of learning to deal with anxiety is figuring out how we can get into fewer of those anxious states in the first place. This subject, confronting anxiety at its source in order to experience less of it, is the focal point of this second section of the book.

As you've probably already experienced, not all anxiety is tied to specific events or moments in time. Sometimes we just get anxious over our financial status or the health of our loved ones. Though our discussion on event-based anxiety will continue throughout our journey together, in this second section of the book, we'll put more of a focus on the anxiety in our lives that isn't bound by time or specific events.

As we flesh out this discussion, we'll talk about what fuels this higher level, non-event-specific anxiety as well as develop lifelong strategies and perspectives for overcoming it. When we finally conclude our time together, my hope is you'll have a set of tools that will help you to not only experience fewer fearful states overall, but also decrease the intensity of those states when they do come knocking. Without further ado, let's begin our discussion by looking at one of the most common sources of non-situation-based anxiety: our school and work life.

ANXIOUS AMERICA

You're sitting at your desk on a Monday afternoon. You can't believe it's only two o'clock. It's been a dreadfully boring day. "I don't think I can stand this for another four days. Someone get me out of here," you say to yourself. As the minutes slowly creep by, your boredom turns into unease. You start to think about why you're even working at this company in the first place. I mean, you're giving it forty hours (or more) of your time every week, and all you feel like you're getting in return is a paycheck.

As you think of all the months that have slipped by at this job, you feel like you're wasting your life. You're confused. Almost everyone grows up and gets a full-time job. Why don't you like yours? And are you crazy if you don't?

If you've ever experienced something like the situation I just described, you're not alone. In fact, according to Gallup's 2017 *State of the Global Workplace* report, only 15% of employees worldwide are engaged at work. Moreover, in the United States, 69% of employees are unhappy with or disengaged at their jobs.[25] Those are staggering numbers. There's a reason why anxiety and depression run rampant in our society and that statistic certainly has something to do with it.

As we talked about in the first part of this book, our brains are constantly on the lookout for threats to our well-being. After all, their main goal is to help us survive. Since our well-being is made up of many parts – not just our physical well-being, but also our emotional, spiritual, and psychological well-being – when something comes along in our lives that threatens any of these areas, our brains go on high alert. While on high alert, we have a tendency to engage in destructive patterns of looping-thinking that perpetuate our anxious symptoms and send us down the rabbit hole.

Even though being disengaged at work seems relatively harmless on the surface, our brains see it differently. To our survival-based brains, there are only two

---

[25] Gallup, Inc., 2017, p. 22, *State of the Global Workplace.*

states in life: falling backward and moving forward; growing and dying. When we mentally check out at work or school but don't find a better place to spend our time, our brains see our disengagement and think, "You are miserable. You are falling behind. This is emotional death. Run for your life."

Sure, it might not always be so obvious, but the feelings of unease we experience when toiling through a job we don't love are our brain's way of telling us this. These feelings are one of the main symptoms of high-level, non-acute anxiety. When we don't listen to them, we risk putting ourselves on high alert for destructively long periods of time.

DISENGAGEMENT TURNED DISMAL

The best example I have of this sort of disengagement-anxiety loop comes from the summer after my sophomore year of college. I'd decided to take an on-campus job where I'd be living and working with a group of my peers to repair furniture in the dorms in preparation for the fall semester. At first, it was kind of fun. We'd wake up early each morning and head to a residential building on campus. There, we'd identify and fix the wobbly chairs, broken shades, and ripped couch cushions in each room.

As the summer wore on, I realized we were quickly running out of things to fix. We had hit every dorm on campus. The days crawled by as we sat in study lounges, waiting for the hours to pass so we could head back to our own rooms.

In college, the summer is pretty long. It starts in early May and runs until early September. My team and I fixed almost everything on campus by mid-June, meaning we still had nearly three months left with little work to do. Day after day, we'd walk around campus, pretending we were headed to a dormitory to repair something in order to appease our bosses. It was such a drag.

By the end of June, the boredom really hit me. I couldn't stand to think about waking up at six a.m. again just to sit around and pretend to work all day. Sure, the hours were decent, the pay was solid, and the workload was a joke. It seemed like every college kid's dream. Except it wasn't.

The boredom turned into disengagement, which turned into a real funk for me. There were very few people on campus besides my coworkers. For one reason or another, several of these coworkers didn't seem to like me. It was quite a trying situation. With each passing day, I felt a bit more dead inside.

Out of that feeling grew negative and anxious patterns of thinking. One day, during that same month of June, an irrational thought popped into my head. It's a bit embarrassing for me to talk about, but it makes for a good example. Sitting in a study lounge, I randomly thought to myself, "I've never had my testicles checked by a doctor. I'm not even sure I've ever checked them myself. What if I had something bad going on down there?" In a state of panic, I rushed to the bathroom and started feeling around, having no idea what I was doing or even looking for. "Oh my god, what the heck is that?!" I said to myself as I came across my epididymis. It didn't feel right. I freaked out.

I was too afraid to google the anatomy of the male body. Instead, I obsessively examined myself for the next few weeks, fearing the worst. The situation finally reached its apex when my roommate walked in on me checking myself in our dorm room. Unfortunately for me, he had no idea what I was *actually* doing. All he knew was I was sitting on my bed with both hands down my pants and my laptop open. When he walked in, I pulled my hands out as fast as I could and tried to defend myself. "It's not what it looks like, I swear!" It's safe to say that was an awkward encounter.

After that moment, I decided I couldn't keep living my life in fear or having my roommate think I was a pervert. I called my doctor and scheduled a check-up. I would have him take a look at what was going on down there and explain the proper way of evaluating myself. Then, one way or another, I'd be able to put this specific bout of anxiety to rest for the time being.

A couple of weeks later, I went in for my appointment, and everything checked out okay. It turned out I was just an anxious mess. I was so pleased and grateful to get the good news. That excitement didn't last long, however. I returned to my boring work arrangement on campus and the disengagement bred new sets of worries.

I knew I couldn't wait for the school year to begin in order to feel alive again. I started brainstorming. I had a car on campus and my friends and family were just twenty miles away. I resolved to start driving home after work so I could spend time with them in the evening. The ninety-minute, rush hour rides in traffic totally sucked, but having fun with my closest pals proved to be a remedy I desperately needed.

I continued going home after work several times a week until fall semester finally arrived. When it did, the excitement of reconnecting with classmates and challenging myself with new courses reinvigorated me. I turned the page on that summer, happy the disengagement was finally gone.

GET SOME PASSION BACK IN YOUR LIFE

So what can we learn from my experience with a less-than-ideal summer job? For starters, whenever we find ourselves spending a lot of time doing something we aren't passionate about, we're eventually going to burn out or feel stuck. That burn out can quickly turn into disengagement and detachment, two familiar homes for anxiety.

When we feel damn near dead inside, our brains can't distinguish the difference between this emotional experience and the physical experience of facing threats to our existence. As such, they bombard us with warning signals, prompting us to change our behavior. Instead of listening to those warning signals, however, we often ignore or push back against them. When we do this, we take away our ability to effectively turn the situation around and, instead, jump right down the anxiety rabbit hole.

What if when we felt disengaged or dead inside, we used those feelings to help us change our situation? Sure, it's not always easy or smart to do so. Leaving a job, relationship, or important situation comes with millions of things to consider: bills to pay, family members to look after, retirement plans, and the like. Luckily, we don't always need to quit our jobs or leave our relationships in order to feel better. All we need to do is find small ways to inject passion into our lives so our brains can feel like they're moving again. This will dampen the survival response they emit, which will help lead us away from our anxious habits.

Injecting passion into our lives need not be a gargantuan task, either. If you're stuck in an accounting job you don't love, but have always wanted to be more creative, you could enroll in a graphic design class after work. If you struggle through long work weeks at your local department store and always envied your rock star cousin, you could sign up for guitar lessons. The bottom line is, when we aren't doing things we're passionate about, we're going to feel disengaged. When we feel this way but don't do anything about it, we open ourselves up to increased levels of anxiety.

This is why it's so important to move ourselves back on the path of passion. In doing so, we attack our anxiety at its source. While this may sound like a daunting task, it's actually pretty easy to get started. All we have to do is take one small step and build momentum. Soon enough, that graphic design course might lead us to something even better: a situation we fully enjoy that doesn't set off our brain's alarms like a blazing fire. However, if you're feeling daring, there's always the more painful, yet shorter experience of *making the jump*. That's the topic we'll discuss in the very next chapter.

MAKING THE JUMP

It was three years after I booked my first skydiving appointment. One of my best friends, Ray, texted our friend group and said that for his birthday, he wanted to go skydiving. He needed some partners in crime. I was torn. I still desperately wanted to jump out of a plane, but had put myself through hell the last time I planned to do so. I couldn't stand the thought of going through that again, and yet, I knew I couldn't keep outrunning the very things I craved doing. With a sense of reckless abandonment, Ray and I booked our appointment for the following month. We were both excited and terrified at the same time.

At this point in my life, I'd already developed a fair amount of the strategies we've discussed in this book so far. The only problem was, I wasn't sure if I'd be able to apply those strategies to a situation I'd already struggled with so much previously. This upcoming jump would surely be a test of that.

I decided the only way I'd be able to get through the skydive would be to live my life as if it were to never arrive. I'd just go about my days as usual, then face whatever fear arose when I got to the edge of that plane – not in the month leading up to it. It wasn't that the risks associated with the skydive didn't exist during that month. It was just that thinking about them would only make me less likely to actually go through with the jump. I knew it wouldn't be easy, but it was the only way.

For the next month, I relentlessly practiced *The Ten Steps*. Then, with the skydive less than twenty-four hours away, I thought back to the 2013 appointment I recounted earlier in this book. I recalled those moments at my house, deep within the bowels of my mind. I remembered how much hell I put myself through by trying to visualize myself successfully jumping out of the plane. Though I was still certainly nervous about the next day's jump, knowing I had avoided that anguish this time around brought a smile to my face. This time, I was actually ready.

The next morning, Ray and I, and a co-worker we recruited the day before, drove up to the northern border of Massachusetts for our appointment. There was no turning back at that point. We arrived at the site early in the morning and checked in at the front desk. The staff told us we'd have to watch a few important safety videos and fill out some forms, then we'd be able to board our plane for our jump.

After the videos and paperwork, we met our instructors and put on our skydiving suits. I told my instructor I was feeling a bit nervous. "Nervous, dude?! I'm fifty years old. I've done over five-thousand jumps in my life. This is just another day at the office for me." Wow. The very thing I was deathly afraid of was also the thing he did twenty times a day, every day. Maybe this wouldn't be so bad after all.

We boarded our tiny, rickety plane and headed into the skies. The instructors all laughed as they messed with us, pretending we'd be jumping by ourselves. Everyone was loose and it made for a hilarious environment. I looked over at my friends. They were both cracking up. There's just something about being eleven-thousand feet in the sky with nerdy goggles on your head that makes you laugh and takes your mind off the task at hand.

One by one, the instructors signaled us to head toward the door of the plane. I watched in amazement as the other members of our group jumped out and rocketed toward the ground below. It was so cool to see. My friends jumped too, and then it was my turn. My instructor and I shimmied our way over to the door where he reminded me how I was supposed to exit the plane. I looked down. This was the moment I had dreaded so much in 2013. Yet, here I was, on a sunny, cheerful day, looking down at our trajectory, ecstatic.

With a rock forward, we propelled ourselves out of the plane and into a somersault. We gracefully rotated in the air until we caught the wind. Then, my instructor and I laughed and took pictures in freefall for the next forty seconds. It was amazing. There's little else out there to make you feel so alive as being one with the sky, speeding toward the ground.

Even in the moment, all the risks I worried about still existed. But when I was finally in that moment, out of my head, those risks didn't hold as much weight. After our forty seconds in freefall, my instructor pulled the cord. We snapped back as our parachute opened, leaving us hanging a mile up in the sky.

I looked around. It was an amazing view. Even from the northern border of Massachusetts, we could still see the Boston skyline. It was breathtaking. As the adrenaline slowed, it hit me. My friends and I had all just done it. We had jumped out of a plane. After another ten minutes or so, we were back on the ground. I ran over to my friends. We all high-fived each other and celebrated a safe journey back to home base.

I turned to find my instructor and have him join in on the celebration. He was already rolling up our parachute and walking back toward the hangar. "That was amazing! How did I do?" I asked him. "Sorry, kid, gotta get back in the plane for my next jump. You did great. Pick up your pictures at the front desk in thirty minutes." Wow. This really was just another day at the office for him. This guy's entire life was predicated on one of the very things I was most afraid of. My instructor shot me a final, big smile, then ran off to his next appointment. That was a dude living his passions despite the risks. It was inspiring.

HOW AND WHY TO JUMP

When we don't engage in our passions in life, we predispose ourselves to anxious habits and thought patterns. While simple acts of passion such as joining an intramural league to play our favorite sport can no doubt help us rediscover that fire within, that passion can be short-lived. Sports leagues end. Semesters draw to a close.

To prevent passion from continuously cycling in and out of our lives, sometimes we need to do something more drastic. Sometimes, we need to shimmy over to the ledge of that plane and make the jump.

I define making the jump as doing something that scares us – something outside of our comfort zones that will shake our lives up for the better or give us a shift in perspective. That jump could be a literal jump like a skydive, or a figurative jump like leaving your job to start your own business.

Whatever that jump might be, it's important to find something that excites and scares you, personally. In doing so, you'll signal to your brain that you're committed to changing and growing. This, in turn, tells your brain to turn off the survival-promoting functions correlated with living a life devoid of inspiration.

So, just how do we jump, and what strategies can we leverage to ensure that we do? While there are many effective methods we could employ, let's focus on a simple, three-part formula. The first part consists of evaluating our current situation and figuring out a way to get ourselves back on the passion path. This is going to look different for everyone. For a college sophomore, this could look like being on the pre-med track only to realize that what you really want to do with your life is give back to your community. With such a realization, you could make the scary transition to a new major, where you might study social work or something similar.

Or, as someone with a job you love, but a lacking friend circle, you could make the realization that, despite your social anxiety, you need to start pushing yourself to get to networking events in order to make new connections. The actual path to passion will be different for everyone. The process will be the same however – you'll identify the parts of your life where passion is missing, resolve to find that passion again, then fully engage in the activities you feel will bring that passion back.

The second part of the formula consists of finding someone who's made a similar jump to the one you seek to carry out. Though I found him through sheer luck rather than an intentional search, meeting my skydive instructor was a real perspective shift for me. Skydiving was something I had always wanted to try, but was too afraid to do. Being paired with him showed me, firsthand, that there are folks out there making a living doing the very things that scare us. Finding someone that fits this mold gives us a mentor of sorts – someone we can emulate and turn to when we have questions about making the jump ourselves.

The third part of the passion formula consists of two essential actions: committing to our jumps and staying out of our heads. Just as a life devoid of passion can lead us to anxiety, so too can a prospective life full of it. This is because most of the things we dream of doing come with risks. Jumping out of an airplane could result in death. Leaving a job to pursue a passion could mean giving up a cushy life in the city and moving back home for a while. These things scare us and often keep us on the passionless path of least resistance. Though these fears are often very real, once we commit to jumping, we have to look away from them and stay out of our heads. If we don't, we might get overwhelmed and keep ourselves stuck on the current path even longer.

Though I've broken it into a simple, three-part formula, making a jump is often more complex. As human beings, we're hardwired to avoid risk and danger. However, the mere fact that we're innately risk-averse doesn't mean we should never seek out new opportunities. The path of least resistance, though comfortable, will rarely lead us to a life of sustained passion and exhilaration. In order to find that exhilaration, we must continually push ourselves into the activities and lifestyles that call us, regardless of how scary they may seem.

HEALTHY DISTRACTION

In a book focused on getting and staying out of our heads, I'd be remiss if I didn't talk about the power of healthy distraction. So often when we're feeling anxious, what's going on inside our minds is we're wrestling with a specific, fear-inducing thought and can't let it go. Though I documented and walked through this phenomenon with *The Ten Steps*, the strategies I outlined in that process were meant to be quickly implementable, in-the-moment tactics. Though engaging in healthy distraction can also be something we do at a moment's notice, its integration into our daily lives is a larger, more holistic process.

In order to preface the concept of healthy distraction, I'd like to look at a common phrase: "Idle hands are the devil's workshop." In essence, this saying implies that when we have little to do, we're likely to engage in activities that can get us into trouble. For example, when I'm bored, some of the first things that cross my mind are, "Turn on the TV. Play video games. Eat a bag of cheese curls. Grab a beer."

I'm not saying we can never engage in these activities, but if we constantly turn to them when we're bored or restless, we're eventually going to find ourselves sick, unmotivated, or out of shape. When we're instead busy or focused on a task we care about, these temptations don't beckon us as often.

Since our thoughts typically drive us to act in specific ways, I've taken this phrase and adapted it to how I understand my mind to work. Thus, when I use this phrase, I typically say, "An idle *mind* is the devil's workshop." That is, when we're disengaged at work, bored at home, or wishing there were more going on in our lives, our anxiety often builds and we become tempted to engage in behaviors that don't empower us.

This kind of logic should sound slightly familiar to you. We've talked about disengagement at length already, both in the previous two chapters and in the chapter on step seven. During our discussion of that seventh step, I asked you to figure out empowering ways to feel good. We talked about leveraging a past memory or a vision of a compelling future to help take your mind off a scary situation you're facing. In this chapter, we'll take that discussion one step further by exploring some of the anxiety-busting lifestyle habits we can adopt as well as some of the science behind one of those strategies.

GET MOVING, GET TALKING

One of the most empowering kinds of healthy distraction is that of physical activity. There are countless forms of it, including playing sports, going for a walk, and weightlifting. It really doesn't matter which form you choose; it's only important that you actually pick one or two you're interested in and commit to them regularly.

Physical activity helps distract us in more ways than one. For starters, when we engage in physical activity, we open ourselves up to new, external stimuli. If we go for a run outside, we may see cars drive by us or bicyclists pedal past us. When we detect these stimuli, we first need to process them, then decide if we're going to focus on any of them. New stimuli, like the ones we may find on an afternoon run, simply don't cross our path when we're sitting at our desks, endlessly obsessing over worst-case scenarios.

Physical activity also distracts us internally. When we exercise, blood flow to our extremities increases. I'm sure you've noticed something like this if you've lifted weights before. Performing bicep curls increases circulation to the muscles in your arm, causing them to feel as though they're increasing in size. This feeling, known as the "pump," is another fantastic, distracting benefit of physical activity.

There's a deeper, more scientific way physical activity distracts us from our negative thinking as well. When we exercise, certain amino acids trigger in our brains, including L-Tryptophan.[26] L-Tryptophan is a precursor of serotonin, a key neurotransmitter that's also known as the happy molecule.[27] Thus, when we exercise, we increase the likelihood that we'll release serotonin and feel good. All of the positive distractions physical activity gives us help break us out of the looping-thinking that gets us into our troublesome, fearful states.

Another form of anxiety-beating, healthy distraction is getting out of the house or office to socialize. I know this is a challenging subject for many of us because socializing, in and of itself, is a great source of anxiety for so many people, myself included. Socializing, when it comes to anxiety, is a paradox, however.

What I mean by that is, the thought of socializing often scares us enough to stop us from doing it, yet at the same time, the very thing we need to do when we're feeling fearful is connect with others and distract ourselves from our worrisome thoughts. Thus, confusingly enough, socializing becomes both the cause of and the remedy for our anxiety.

When we find ourselves stuck in this paradox, we must use *The Ten Steps* to get out of our heads and then just get out there and socialize anyway. Even something as simple as going out with your best friend and grabbing a sandwich or coffee can be a mind-freeing exercise. The very act of conversing with another person is something that requires focus and pushes us to drop the burdensome thoughts swirling in our minds, even if only momentarily.

The opposite of socializing, living in isolation, is far less likely to distract us from our negative thoughts. When we isolate ourselves for too long, we step into the wrestling ring with nothing other than our mental demons. As we've

---

[26] Amen, Daniel G. "Getting Unstuck: Cingulate System Prescriptions." Change Your Brain, Change Your Life: The Breakthrough Program for Conquering Anxiety, Depression, Obsessiveness, Anger, and Impulsiveness, Three Rivers Press, 1998, p. 185.
[27] Jenkins, Trisha A, et al. "Influence of Tryptophan and Serotonin on Mood and Cognition with a Possible Role of the Gut-Brain Axis." Nutrients, vol. 8, no. 1, 20 Jan. 2016, doi:10.3390/nu8010056.

seen throughout this book, fighting against them rarely gets us anywhere.

Even though it can be quite difficult at times, push yourself to get in the habit of leaving the house and socializing when you're feeling anxious. I've struggled to do this in the past and have learned, the hard way, that the depths of my mind are typically far scarier than interacting with other people. This realization has helped me get out and mingle when I'm feeling down.

PLANNING YOUR DISTRACTIONS

When we stay stuck in our anxiety-provoking patterns of looping-thinking, we cut ourselves off from potential changes in perspective that taking a break or engaging in a new experience could provide us. For example, even though we may know pausing from stressful work to grab lunch with a friend could be the very reset we need, we don't always give ourselves that break. Thus, the very thing we need to do becomes the very thing we won't do, which only causes our stress to build upon itself and make us feel even worse.

Even more ironic, sometimes when we actually do say yes to empowering distractions, such as invites out with friends, we realize just how stress-relieving these experiences can be, promise to commit to them regularly, and then fail to do so again and again. We often make this blunder not because we're lazy, irrational, or unmotivated, but because our anxious, one-track minds frequently distract us from the potential benefits such a rendezvous could provide us. We can't have our mental state hinge upon the chance that we'll feel good enough to engage in regular, empowering distraction. In order to ensure that we participate in said activities continually, we must schedule them.

There are several types of empowering distractions we can schedule. We'll talk about two here. The first is the kind of short, frequent break from monotonous or stressful work that helps us get back into our bodies and out of whatever mental task we're currently performing. These are the quick walks down the hall or set of twenty jumping jacks at our desks. Though they're short, they're effective when performed regularly. When working, studying, or engaging in any other activity that requires a good amount of mental effort, we should schedule them every hour, at a minimum, so we don't fall down the depths of our minds.

When I say these activities should be planned, I mean you should have some mechanism that reminds you to take part in them. There are countless tools on the market you can leverage to make these healthy distractions a part of your daily life. For example, you can use the calendar application on your smartphone to alert you on a regular interval. Or, you can download a desktop or mobile application that exists for this very purpose.

Search for the term "focus boosting" on the App Store or Google Play Store and you'll find several helpful applications. I've used iOS apps such as *Focus Keeper*, *Stand Up!*, and *Focus Booster* in the past. All of these kinds of products are designed to help us engage in planned, healthy distraction. Such distraction makes it easier for us to switch gears and get out of our heads when we need it most.

The second type of activity we can schedule is what I call an *accountability activity*. I use that term because these types of scheduled events are inherently more difficult to cancel once scheduled; this is because cancelling them can cost us, be it in social capital or physical currency. These kinds of activities are the non-refundable fitness classes, the restaurant reservations out with friends, and other events we must commit to in some capacity before putting them on the calendar.

If we make a reservation for lunch with a friend and want to cancel, we need to call the restaurant in order to do so. Though not terribly difficult, the prospective act of calling the restaurant provides friction that prevents us from just bailing at a moment's notice. In addition, if we cancel on our friend, it's likely he or she will be disappointed with us.

This potential disappointment can fuel us to stick to our commitments, despite how busy we are with our work or how stressed we're feeling that day. That feeling of potentially letting a friend down keeps us accountable to follow through with what we said we'd do. Even though we may not always want to carry out these commitments, we need them on our calendars. Events we can cancel without any potential ramifications don't provide us the push we need to engage in healthy distraction.

While distracting ourselves for a minute each hour or having lunch with a friend may seem more like an in-the-moment strategy for dealing with our anxiety, the truth is, in order for such a strategy to be effective for us, we need to make these breaks a part of our hourly and daily lives. Doing so conditions our behavior long-term and helps us get in grooves that keep us out of the deep tracks of our fear-focused minds.

THE ULTIMATE DISTRACTION

The final type of distraction I want to discuss is what I consider to be the ultimate form of it. That very form is the practice of setting and driving toward personal goals. This distraction practice is the most important type because the pursuit of a specific aim guides our behavior and gives us a consistent subject to focus on, especially when we feel scared.

As you'll recall, I've made a few references to the idea of sitting at a desk, performing a boring, potentially soul-sucking job throughout this book. Such jobs are the antithesis of what driving toward real goals should feel like. Without giving us a target to move toward, these kinds of jobs keep us stuck in the bowels of our minds. In order to stay out of those dark places, we need a major, empowering distraction. We need a goal that excites us, dictates our actions, and motivates us to keep moving.

Let's say, for example, you have a goal of starting a curated clothing website. You give yourself three months to negotiate deals with manufacturers, create some basic marketing materials, and build the site itself. Each of these tasks requires a vast amount of effort and dictates what your day-to-day will look like. For example, you may start your mornings with calls to potential partner companies, spend lunch working on campaign emails and advertisements, and burn the midnight oil putting the site together.

The goal itself helps you stay focused by giving you clear, defined tasks to perform and a target to hit. When different things in your life come up that push you toward engaging in looping-thinking, you can remember the end goal of launching your site. In doing so, you'll remind yourself of the different tasks you must first complete, which should give you something to keep busy with and focus on.

I know I must always have something I'm striving toward that provides me with a focused, purposeful busyness. I learned this lesson late in college. Even with a full class schedule, the amount of time I spent in the classroom wasn't terribly burdensome. Five classes only required about twelve hours of lectures a week. Though homework and studying for tests certainly demanded some additional time, I still often had six to eight free hours a day. My friends and I usually spent those hours playing video games, eating unhealthy foods, and sleeping way too late.

While these activities were fun in small doses, they made me feel purposeless and stressed out when they were the focal point of my days. It wasn't until later on in college that I realized I needed to use my time more wisely. Senior year, I threw myself into the creation of an iPhone game. It was the first project in college I truly cared about, and it helped me feel like I wasn't just throwing away some of the best years of my life.

Without a passion project, goal, or side hustle, I often feel like I'm drifting along without a purpose. This lack of purposeness is the very reason we feel stressed or anxious when stuck in roles and jobs we don't care about. Avoiding these feelings is what pushes so many people to dedicate themselves to causes and missions they find important.

If you aren't working toward a specific goal currently, I ask that you spend some time thinking of one you could shoot for that would help keep you invigorated and focused. It could be business-related or something entirely different, like learning a new language. Whatever it may be, just make sure it's time-stamped and something you're passionate about. Without a defined finish line, it's much harder to hold ourselves accountable with completing our goals, let alone measure how much progress we're making on them.

Without something to shift our focus from the thoughts that scare us most, our minds will keep gravitating toward those very thoughts. If we don't have something uplifting to focus on, it becomes quite difficult to direct that focus somewhere positive. That's exactly why planning empowering distractions and setting invigorating goals, both large and small, is so important in managing anxiety.

As you make empowering distraction a part of your everyday life, you'll give yourself a chance to break free from the potential outcomes and possibilities that scare and grip you the most. The more you make said practice a part of your routine, the more you'll condition your mind to stop looking at these outcomes, which should only help drive your anxiety down, long-term.

WHAT'S REALLY DRIVING YOU?

In thinking critically about anxiety throughout this book, we've sought to answer the question of *why*. Why does our anxiety proliferate in certain situations but dissipate in others? When pondering what it is that drives us to do anything, this ultimate question of *why* is inevitable.

It's not easy to make sense of why we do many of the things we do. Just evaluating our behaviors at face value doesn't always explain our underlying motivations. In order to discover those motivations, we must look deeper than our surface-level behaviors. We must explore the needs responsible for driving those actions.

Humans are pre-programmed to seek out a myriad of different means. We're driven to find jobs, relationships, and places to live, just to name a few. In the world of psychology, these means would be described as vehicles for the attainment of various ends. Those ends, most often called human needs, are the building blocks of motivation, the forces that drive our decisions and behaviors.

The subject of human needs has been a focal point of psychological research in the twentieth and twenty-first centuries. One of the most popular theories on human needs developed during this time period is that by Abraham Maslow, aptly titled *Maslow's Hierarchy of Needs*.

In his 1943 paper, *A Theory of Human Motivation*, Maslow outlines what he believes to be the core needs of mankind. He explains how our needs for physiological well-being, safety, love, self-esteem, and self-actualization influence our behavior in hierarchical form.[28] That is, we prioritize, and seek out, our need for water before our need to feel proud. Maslow's theory was unquestionably groundbreaking and influential, but in modern times, where we are free, for the most part, of the perils of life in the wild, it seems slightly outdated.

What I mean by that is, in today's society, many of us have our physiological and safety needs met, yet we don't spend all of our waking hours only searching for the remaining three (love, self-esteem, and self-actualization). While those needs certainly play a role in our day-to-day lives, in my opinion, they don't totally capture all of the other forces that drive our behavior.

As such, I'd like to propose to modify Maslow's hierarchy a bit. In the following section, I'll describe a slightly more modern take on Maslow's theory and explain how some of the needs in it influence our actions regularly. As we step through some of those needs in more detail, we'll see how our pursuit of them can influence the amount of anxiety we feel in our everyday lives.

REWRITING MASLOW'S HIERARCHY OF NEEDS

When I learned of Maslow's hierarchy in a high school psychology class, I felt like something was missing. I wondered which of the needs he outlined could justify my desire to go to the driving range, watch football, or engage in any other relatively harmless, fun activity. It wasn't until I began writing this book that I revisited his theory and outlined a new set of drives I believe to be more inclusive. I've spelled my new set out below. Take a read through them, then we'll apply the most relevant ones to our battles with anxiety.

1. **Physiological needs**: our core, primal needs including air, water, sleep, food, and exercise. Without meeting these needs, we would, quite literally, cease to exist.

---

[28] Maslow, Abraham H. "A Theory of Human Motivation." *Psychological Review*, July 1943, pp. 370–396., doi:10.1037/h0054346.

2. **Security**: our need to feel safe in our surroundings and sure of ourselves. If we didn't feel secure in our environment, it would be very difficult for us to function properly. We'd constantly be battling fears, worries, and countless other uncertainties.

3. **Love**: our need to feel like we belong in our environment and are connected to those around us. We all crave love in some fashion, whether we knowingly understand it or not. It's the very thing that drives us to make friends, get into relationships, and share our experiences with one another.

4. **Novelty**: our need to experience new things. If every day of our lives were exactly the same, we'd eventually get bored. Novelty works in both the short-term and the long-term. It's this need that drives us to try exotic foods, travel to new places, and switch jobs.

5. **Expression**: our need to project our self-image into the world around us. We express ourselves through the words we use, the clothes we wear, the products we buy, the music we listen to, and so on. When we don't express ourselves, we feel bottled up. It's our need to express our internal world to the external world that helps us come alive.

6. **Importance**: our need to feel different and special. Our desire to feel special is the very thing that pushes us to apply to prestigious universities, buy designer goods, and climb the corporate ladder. It helps us stand out from the crowd and be recognized.

7. **Growth**: our need to feel like we're becoming more than we currently are, like we're progressing toward something. In nature, organisms either grow or die. There is no in-between. Our need to progress keeps us alive. It's this need that drives us to learn new skills and take on larger responsibilities.

8. **Impact**: our need to make our mark on our environment through our actions. Our need for impact is what I would call our desire for immortality. Making a difference in the world or improving the lives of those around us makes us feel like we might live on in the hearts of others, long after our departure from this world.

Though the changes I've made seem large at first, Maslow's original needs still shine through quite a bit. For starters, the second need on my list, security, is a modification of Maslow's second need, safety. In my eyes, the word safety doesn't reach far enough. While it helps classify our desire to quickly walk past an aggressively barking dog, it doesn't do as good of a job explaining our decisions in less threatening situations. For example, staying at a job we don't enjoy so we can pay our bills. In my mind, calling this second need security, instead of safety, explains such conflicting desires more clearly.

Secondly, just like Maslow's original list, mine includes love at the number three spot. Seventy-five years after Maslow's original publication, not much has changed in regard to this need. Humans are still one of the most altricial species on earth. Without a loving parent or guardian by our side at birth and throughout infancy, we simply wouldn't survive. Once we develop the ability to fend for ourselves, both our self-love and our connections with others keep us alive by pushing us to engage in activities that will boost our spirits and help us grow.

From there, my list starts to deviate from Maslow's a bit. There are quite a few reasons for this. The first is, I feel as though Maslow's need, self-esteem, doesn't paint the whole picture. Sure, we all want to feel good about ourselves and our abilities, but, in my opinion, self-esteem is a means to an end. That end is security, and one of the ways we find it is through one of our other needs – self-expression. As we express ourselves to the world, we come to understand ourselves better and become more confident.

Secondly, the final need in Maslow's list, self-actualization, is really a fancy way of saying that we're striving to become the best versions of ourselves. Like self-esteem, in my opinion, self-actualization is a bit too much of an umbrella or catch-all. That is, it seeks to cover several needs at once and doesn't intuitively explain human behavior as well as breaking it apart might.

It's my belief that we become the best versions of ourselves through several needs. That is, we learn through novel situations and use the love and guidance others provide us to grow into, and realize, our full potentials on earth. On our way to our full potentials, we continually grow so we can continually make an impact on our world. The combination of all of these needs, specifically growth and impact, is the reason I feel it necessary to divide self-actualization into multiple parts.

While we could certainly talk about the differences between my list and Maslow's for quite some time, my goal is not to bore you with semantics. Instead, it's to introduce you to an easy-to-follow framework for explaining human behavior so we can see why seeking certain needs sometimes leads us to do things that aren't always healthy or helpful for us. Now that we've covered that framework, I think we're finally ready to discuss how these needs play a role in our experience of anxiety.

THE LIGHT AND DARK SIDES OF SECURITY

Unlike Maslow's list of needs, I don't consider my version to follow a hierarchy. Sure, we all need air, water, sleep, and food before we can do much of anything else. But once we've attained those fundamental needs, in my opinion, we can seek out our remaining needs in any order we so choose.

That's not to say I didn't order my list in a specific fashion, it's just that my list is a suggestion more than it is a mandate. What I mean by this is, for example, most of us want to feel some sense of security before we seek to make an impact on our world. The amount of security each of us needs in order to make that impact varies, however. The same concept applies when talking about our needs in general – we must all meet each need on *some* level, but the degree to which we do differs from person to person.

In my mind, this, at least partially, explains why we all have different personalities; each of our characters is shaped by how much we value each of our individual needs. For example, an introvert may care more about feeling secure and expressing him or herself than an extrovert, who might instead value connecting with others and seeking out novel situations more highly.

Just like we can hypothesize how an introvert or an extrovert might value certain needs over others, so too can we attempt to explain how someone with an anxious personality values his or her own needs. From my experience in dealing with my own anxiety, I would say there are two specific needs most strongly correlated with an anxious personality: security and importance. We'll start with the former.

Uncertainty is the only certain thing in life. Our favorite restaurants could close at any moment. We could get fired from our jobs tomorrow. The stock market could tank next week. There's no way of ever knowing what will happen in our lives. We can only truly know that change is constant.

If you recall my *Three Tenets of Anxiety*, you'll remember that the first tenet states, "All anxiety is rooted in uncertainty." That is, what makes us anxious is often our inability to accept the fact that we cannot know how most things in our lives will turn out. When we place too much value on our need for security, we subconsciously fight back against this inevitable uncertainty. That sort of behavior, as we've seen, is one of the habits that sinks us deep down the rabbit hole.

That's certainly not to say security isn't important. It's just that in today's modern society, we probably don't need as much of it as our prehistoric, survival-based brains are used to seeking out. If we lived in a war zone, we'd be in constant fear for our lives, and justifiably so. That fear would force us to focus on, and figure out, a way of escaping the chaotic environment, at any cost. In these sorts of situations, our need for security pushes us to find our way out of the danger. In time, getting back to a safe environment typically leads us to step out of our comfort zones in order to find new opportunities and seek out our other needs.

However, sometimes even after finding security, we still want more of it. This can be toxic. When we continually place too much value on our need for security, we predispose ourselves to the kind of thoughts and actions that typically lead to anxiety.

For example, on the hunt to feel secure, we may wait until we're totally certain before starting that business we've always wanted to. Or, driven by the same power, we may try to control the people, events, and happenings in our lives. The reason why clinging to security can be so dangerous is that there are so many things in our lives we cannot control. Trying to control these things only keeps us stuck where we are, anxiously questioning why we aren't moving forward. Often, that place we get stuck is somewhere deep within our fear-based minds.

Given that we all value security differently, there's no one-size-fits-all solution for suddenly changing the amount we feel we need in order to function properly. However, sometimes a simple reminder of how we can find security helps us seek out and satisfy our craving for this need more easily.

There are countless ways by which we can meet this need. For example, we can find it in knowing our home safety systems are armed, protecting our possessions and loved ones. We can also find security in our morning cup of tea or coffee, which might provide us the certainty that we'll be able to power through our day successfully. The ultimate form of security, however, comes from within. Often, we develop that internal sense of security through experience.

What I mean by that is, as we get older and weather more mental storms, we build our strength and resilience. We come to realize just how many dangerous or uncertain situations we've made it through. As we reconnect to this realization, we can remind ourselves that throughout all of those situations, we didn't know how things would play out, yet we figured out how to handle the corresponding outcomes anyway, even if they initially looked frightening.

Reconnecting to our ability to "figure it out" helps us see that it's our own internal resourcefulness, not our ability to predict the future, that typically determines where we end up in life. Knowing this helps us realize just how treacherous an incessant need for security can be in regard to our anxiety. As we combine these realizations, we increase the amount of security we feel internally as well as lower the amount that we feel is necessary from our outside world.

This kind of thinking helps prepare us to deal with many of the challenges we'll face in the future. It also helps us see the effect that the prioritization of our own needs has on how we think and feel. Similarly, and most importantly, it gives us a powerful, permanent tool in the constant struggle of staying out of our heads.

SEEKING IMPORTANCE IN THE WRONG PLACES

We all want to feel important on some level. Just like our need for security, there's nothing inherently wrong with wanting to feel special. In fact, it's part of our very nature. Standing out from the crowd can help us get ahead in life, be it through better financial resources, a richer education, or an extended social network.

All of these displays of importance are attractive to our survival-based brains. On some level, we equate standing out with survival of the fittest. As we boost our standing in society, we, even if only subconsciously, signal to ourselves that we're avoiding being the odd man out. Yet while we all need to feel important or special on some level, the ways about which most of us try to fulfill this need are often backward. That backwardness is another way we invite anxiety into our lives.

For many of us, seeking importance might mean chasing high-paying careers, prestigious job titles, or degrees from top-notch universities. Not all of us will get into those schools or achieve a high level of wealth, yet all of us must still find ways to satisfy our need to feel special. This, in and of itself, creates conflict within many of us. For example, if we realize that we've been unsuccessful at achieving importance through "traditional" channels such as wealth or fame, we might start to look for other ways to stand out. Not all of those ways leave us feeling alive or empowered, however.

Let me give you an example. Larry is thirty years old and experiences a good amount of anxiety as well as the occasional panic attack. He often feels debilitated by his condition and is reluctant to talk to anyone about it. Ask him today, and he'll tell you he hasn't yet excelled in the areas of his life he deems most important. He sees both his career and social life as lackluster. One day, however, Larry decides to seek help for his anxiety. He contacts a local medical professional, Dr. Smith, to make an appointment.

At the appointment, Dr. Smith asks Larry some questions about his condition. Thirty minutes pass, and the doctor feels he hasn't made much progress with Larry. He knows he must keep pushing. He asks Larry what the worst part of his anxiety is, to which Larry exclaims, "Will you stop pestering me already? You have no idea what it's like to experience this day in and day out! My anxiety is just downright brutal!" On the surface, it might not sound like much, but this admission tells the doctor quite a bit about how Larry sees his condition.

Dr. Smith has studied the work of Abraham Maslow and is well-versed in the areas of human needs and motivation. He uses Larry's answers to hypothesize that Larry meets his need for importance not through fancy titles or relationships but through his anxiety. As you could probably imagine, using a debilitating condition to meet one's needs isn't very empowering.

In fact, it's one of the main things holding Larry back from making progress with his condition. Whether Larry knows it or not, his anxiety serves him on some level – the fact that no one can understand him or his condition helps him feel, even if only subconsciously, a bit special. If he were to rid himself of it, he'd need to find more empowering ways to feel important in order to prevent himself from regressing to his anxious ways.

Dr. Smith, having seen this kind of case before, makes some suggestions to Larry. One of his suggestions is to have Larry start an anxiety peer group in his neighborhood. Larry mentioned how several neighbors told him they experience anxiety themselves, so he'd likely have a few members right off the bat. In starting this group, the doctor hypothesizes, Larry will be able to connect with other people going through the same thing he is. This might, in turn, help him discover some important strategies for dealing with his own condition.

In time, Dr. Smith mentions, Larry could expand his peer group by inviting members to bring friends or by hosting more frequent meetings. As this group grows and its members make strides with their struggles, Larry could take pride in knowing he's at least partially responsible for all of those strides. "What a wonderful way to feel important," Larry thinks.

Dr. Smith knows starting such a peer group could be very scary for Larry, however. As such, he makes some other helpful recommendations as well. For example, he tells Larry that by picking up a new hobby, like tennis or chess, he could give his mind something to think about other than the anxiety. In time, getting better at this new hobby might help Larry feel a bit more special as well.

The number of ways by which Larry could meet his need for importance in empowering fashion is limitless. By moving away from using his anxiety as a way to feel important, Dr. Smith suggests, it's likely Larry will not only experience less anguish overall, but also find excitement in picking up these new hobbies and forming deeper relationships.

RETHINKING THE VALUE WE PLACE ON EACH OF OUR NEEDS

We all assign different values to the innate, human needs we have. Typically, we assign those values subconsciously. That is, we don't usually sit down at a predefined point in our lives and say, "I want to live primarily in pursuit of love and growth." However, we can rethink, even change, the value we place on each of our needs, if we so choose. This is how we can create long-lasting personality shifts. All it takes is a little leverage.

In order for us to change the value we've assigned to each of our needs, we must have a compelling reason for doing so. Without seeing how our need-value choices are hindering us, there will be little incentive to change them. Since anxiety typically stems from our need for both security and importance, and we've already covered the potential pitfalls associated with those needs, I hope those possible hindrances are now clear.

The reason why identifying incentives for changing our need-value choices is important is that said incentives will fuel us to follow through with our promises and pull us toward the life we desire. For example, if anxiety holds us back in social situations, reevaluating how we prioritize our needs might give us the leverage required to stop valuing security so highly and instead start valuing novelty or love, more. In doing so, we may find ourselves opening up in social situations despite how scared we feel in them.

Once we've identified the ways our most highly prioritized needs hold us back and uncovered incentives for changing the prioritization of those needs, the next thing we must do in order to make our reordering last is find new, more empowering ways to meet the very needs we wish to deprioritize.

For example, it can be very difficult to stop a habit like eating junk food. Instead of just not indulging, we have to replace that habit with a new, more beneficial one. Without doing so, we're likely to stress ourselves out – just think about what not being able to eat the donuts in your pantry would feel like if you simultaneously weren't allowed to do something to get your mind off those tasty treats.

An example of a replacement behavior in this situation would be telling ourselves that whenever we feel the urge to open the snack drawer, we'll either go for a walk around the block or eat a piece of fruit. Both of these actions would be stimulating on some level, and would likely help us feel better about ourselves than eating the junk food would.

Once you come up with some empowering ways to meet the needs you wish to devalue, you'll have everything required for carrying out a full reprioritization of the driving forces behind your behaviors. It's my hope that, in time, such a reprioritization will lead you away from your anxious tendencies and move you toward new, exciting experiences. To make what I'm saying a bit more concrete, I'll walk you through what it might look like if you were to implement this process in your own life.

Let's say you work at a law firm where the days tend to drag on slowly. Up to today, you've always subconsciously valued security and importance quite highly, and as such, you've developed a tendency to get in your head at times and worry about things you can't control. Even though you love the paychecks, you know the mundane days at this job are only contributing to your overthinking and anxiety.

Having just read my take on Maslow's needs hierarchy, you decide to evaluate your own needs and see how they've influenced the choices you've made in your career thus far. As you complete your evaluation, you realize your need to feel secure and important in life led you to this prestigious firm, its lofty titles, and its fine paychecks. Though you certainly enjoy those things and are reluctant to give them up, you also know they aren't totally fulfilling.

You've always been an adventurer. You dream of taking weeks off at a time and traveling to tropical climates where you can surf. Unfortunately, your company doesn't let you take off more than one week in a row. As you do some introspection, you realize your adventurous side is really your need for novelty in action. You love being in new places, meeting new people, and letting loose on the waves. Unfortunately, your legal lifestyle doesn't lend itself to those experiences often.

The thought of leaving your job makes you even more anxious than a typical, boring day at your desk does. You wonder what you'd do without a steady income stream. You also wonder, however, how miserable you'd be if you spent another year of your life trapped in your cubicle, not living the bold lifestyle you've always dreamed of.

All of these feelings combine to make you realize that while your desire to feel secure and important has been driving your life as of late, it doesn't make you feel alive. You remember being in college, studying abroad, where you were learning and growing every day. Man, how great that made you feel. You resolve to get back to a life of novelty and growth. But first, you need a strategy for getting there.

You brainstorm a list of new ways to meet your now devalued needs – security and importance – then apply the same process to the ones you just put at the top of your list – novelty and growth. After some thinking, you hone in on one of those ideas. You decide maybe you could dust off your old bartending skills and put them to good use. You figure that working your way up to be lead bartender at the fanciest steakhouse in town could help you redevelop that sense of importance you've found in your comfortable, albeit unfulfilling, job.

But that still leaves three needs unmet. You look down at the list you brainstormed and realize bartending comes with a less rigorous schedule than a job at a law firm does. In your old job as a waiter, you took three weeks off at a time to backpack various countries in Central and South America. Being able to do so again, this time as a bartender, would not only expose you to loads of new adventures, but also help you feel secure in knowing your next journey is never too far away.

Sure, maybe that sense of security wouldn't be as strong as the feelings you get from your generous paychecks, but the hustle and bustle of working at a new restaurant would help keep you out of your head. You resolved to stop living in pursuit of so much security in the future anyway, and feel as though the promise of a situation with less anxiety surrounding it is all you need right now, even if the paychecks aren't as big.

In the days that follow, you interview at top steakhouses in your city and eventually land a bartending job. You leave your law firm a few weeks later, giving yourself a two-week gap between gigs to head to California and do some surfing. You're not exactly sure where this journey will take you, but, empowered with a new appreciation for novelty and growth, you remember to let the need to know how things will turn out fall by the wayside.

While the example we just walked through is a hypothetical one, I don't think it's too big of a stretch to say you could apply a similar exercise in your own life. In fact, I know many people, myself included, who've done this very thing. It can be an extremely rewarding process.

As we think about the value we place on each of our needs and how those needs influence where we end up in life, we should remember that a desire for security and importance often keeps us stuck on the anxiety path. That's not to say those needs aren't important. It's just that anxiety helps us meet them quite easily, so if we're not careful, chasing those two needs first can predispose us to living out our fears. As such, we should strive to live in pursuit of our other needs, or at the very least, more empowering ways to find security and importance.

Before we fly off to the next chapter, I invite you to participate in this need-value reprioritization exercise. Take a look and the needs you value highest and the ways by which you meet those needs. From there, ask yourself if reprioritizing your needs or meeting those needs in different ways might prove beneficial in your internal struggles. Deciding who you want to become is up to you, and it starts with the kind of thinking we've outlined in this chapter.

FOCUS ON GROWTH

A few months after my friend Tess returned to the US, I hit a bump in the road. She and I went out a couple of times, but ultimately, it didn't work out. I was coming to terms with that, and knew it wasn't the end of the world, but still struggled to get through it. On top of that, my job was still as boring as it had been while she was traveling. I had no escape plan, no compelling vision for the future, and few things scheduled in my life to be excited about. I felt stuck.

While she was away, I developed much of the framework for this book, and that was a huge source of personal growth for me. But, despite that growth while she was gone, it wasn't enough to get me through the months following her return. In order to weather that next difficult time period, I knew I needed to replicate that growth again, this time in other areas of my life.

When Tess returned, she and I talked about how much her trip helped her grow as a person. Seeing new places, facing challenges, and making friends with strangers in foreign lands made her feel much more competent than she'd previously given herself credit for. She described, and showed, a renewed sense of confidence and lust for life. Whatever she wanted to call it, I was envious and wanted some of it for myself.

I'd always enjoyed traveling but hadn't done a lot of it internationally. Seeing what her trip did for her pushed me into planning an adventurous, growth-promoting trip of my own. About a month after we parted ways, I booked a twenty-three-day trip around Portugal, France, and Spain and couldn't have been more excited. That was, until the trip actually neared.

Fast forward about six months. My travels were less than a week away. In the weeks leading up to that one, I jumped all the way inside my head. I couldn't stop trying to picture myself on the trip. I couldn't stop asking myself questions that kept me thinking in circles. How would I be able to take seven international flights by myself? I don't like flying. What if I didn't make any friends? What if I got mugged or kidnapped? These questions weren't helpful, but they were difficult to silence.

A couple of days before I left for my trip, things got worse. I was at the gym after work and looked up at the television. CNN was reporting that a plane flying out of Charles De Gaulle airport in France had gone down with no survivors. Officials couldn't tell if the crash was due to a mechanical failure or foul play.

"Add that to the list of terrible things happening in Paris these days, including the November 2015 terrorist attacks, and I'd question whether it's even safe to travel here right now," said one of the news anchors. I'd be flying into and out of CDG airport at the end of my trip. I wondered if the broadcaster was right.

On Friday of that same week, I went out with some friends and we drunkenly joked about how unsafe Europe had been as of late. "I just imagine myself walking from café to café and there being someone running down the street, shooting them all up. I could never bring myself to go. I'd be way too scared of something like that happening," said one of my friends.

I knew my concerns were unfounded. Acts of violence and terror could just as easily happen in any major US city. But still, I had to hide how anxious the conversation made me. Deep down, I was losing my mind. I was leaving for Portugal the next day. I had no idea how I'd get through the first flight, let alone the twenty-three-day journey.

I woke up the next morning and started packing. I was so anxious. I'd promised my parents I'd visit before I left, so I stopped by their house. I told them I was very nervous and they helped me calm down a bit. They reminded me this was a trip I desperately wanted to take, the one I had been looking forward to for so long. They told me that one bad story about one plane overlooked the fact that tens of thousands of flights land safely in Europe every day. It was a very helpful conversation. As I left their house, I hugged them and thanked them for their support.

On my way to the airport, I stopped at a store for some snacks. As I exited that store, I looked down at my phone and saw I had a voicemail from my aunt. She'd remembered I was leaving that day and called to wish me safe travels. "I was thinking of you and your trip. I know it's probably a pretty stressful day today. Just remember you're going to have an amazing time! Stay safe and send lots of pictures!" It was as if she had read my mind. I called her right back.

I told her how I was feeling and she helped me move through it. "I know you're really nervous today, but think about what this trip means to you and how much fun you'll have once you get there." She paused. "I know it's not easy to push yourself and live the life you want. But that's the only way to do it. Thanks for giving my kids someone to look up to. We can't wait to hear all about your trip. It's going to be awesome." I thanked her for the amazingly kind words, hung up the phone, and started bawling my eyes out. The magnitude of the day overwhelmed me. Her words looped in my head. *It's not easy to push yourself and live the life you want.* No, it's not. But that can never stop us.

When I finally got to the airport, I was still a bit of a mess. I walked through the doors and went right to the bathroom. It was really sinking in. I was about to go to Europe by myself for almost a month. I splashed some water on my face and took a deep breath, then headed for security. After getting through TSA, I went right to the bar. I needed it.

I'd been leveraging *The Ten Steps* that day, but, given the magnitude of the trip, felt like I needed another push. I made a few friends as I gulped down two glasses of red wine. Both the friends and the alcohol made me feel better. Less than an hour later, with the help of the wine, I boarded my midnight flight for Portugal. I found my seat and, much to my surprise, fell asleep before takeoff. When I awoke, we were in Europe.

Despite some difficulties with the language, I found my hostel and quickly hit my stride. I met tons of new friends, ate lots of delicious foods, and took in some amazing sights. I trekked from Portugal to France to Spain and back to France again. It was a fulfilling trip. There's nothing like doing the thing your soul calls you to do, whatever that may be.

I returned home with a sense of pride for having pushed myself into the uncertainties of journeying through a continent solo. It was a good feeling. After that trip, I returned to Europe twice more that summer, without the dread and anxiety that accompanied me the first time around.

Truth be told, the first time I landed in Europe, almost all of my fears dissipated. As we've discussed, the time leading up to an anxiety-provoking situation is often the most difficult part to get through – not the situation itself. Once we're in the moment we've been fearing, we often find that our presence returns and our fears subside. Sure, there are exceptions to every rule, but even in advance of situations we dread entirely, the depths of our minds are typically much scarier than anything we'll ever face for real.

The reason I told that story is to show you that growth can be found *through* anxiety. I'm sure you've heard the expression, "Our greatest desires lie on the other side of our biggest fears." We fear the things we care about most because those things can affect us immensely in either the positive or negative direction. Solo trips to Europe can be exhilarating, soul-searching experiences, but they can also be dangerous. Though our brains may see danger and immediately tell us to start running, we sometimes have to push through that response. The only way we can do this is by seeing anxiety differently – not as an inhibitor or thing to be feared, but as a sign growth is right around the corner.

ANXIETY, THE GROWTH GAUGE

I'm sure you've also heard the expression *practice makes perfect*. Though it's a bit of a cliché, it relates back to anxiety quite well. The more anxiety-provoking, yet objectively safe, situations we put ourselves in, the more we learn how to handle the anxiety associated with those situations. When we push ourselves out of our comfort zones and challenge ourselves to take on new responsibilities, we become different people. We pick up new strategies and gain confidence. This confidence, in turn, allows us to take on even greater challenges.

From my experience, the largest impediment to us taking up these challenges is the belief that anxious symptoms are signals something is wrong. When we subscribe to this belief, we forget that our fight-or-flight systems exist for two reasons: to help us flee threatening situations *or* battle through them.

The increased adrenaline, cortisol, and blood flow you experience during anxious situations can help prepare your body to perform better and react more efficiently to the very things that frighten you. Improved performance, in turn, often helps us reach new levels of skill and achievement. If we constantly run away from these feelings or sensations when they present themselves, we may never experience that growth.

Thus, we must start viewing our anxiety as a gauge for growth. When our anxious symptoms arise from situations free of real, physical threats, we must not turn and run immediately, but instead see those symptoms for what they really are – indications that we're beyond our comfort zone, the place where growth occurs.

Exposing ourselves to newer and more challenging things is how we've grown throughout our lives. In school, we moved from one grade to the next by learning new concepts and continuously applying those ideas to more intricate and complex problems. If we didn't open ourselves up to those new experiences, we wouldn't have advanced. The same goes for exposing yourself to your anxiety. If you start small, you'll eventually get the little wins you need to level up. Over time, those wins add up and turn into huge victories and growth.

But what are we to do about the negative potential outcomes from situations that scare us? Change the way we see them. After all, frightening possibilities aren't what make us anxious – it's our perception of those possibilities.

As we start to view them in a different light, we'll see our anxiety in a different manner as well. Once we come to view negative potential outcomes, and the anxiety surrounding them, as catalysts for learning and growth rather than threats to our survival, we'll more willingly push ourselves into fear-inducing situations.

I know it might sound a bit far-fetched, but negative outcomes and disappointments truly are vehicles for personal growth. Even though they're difficult to go through and experience, they often serve as our greatest teachers in life. Can you think of such a disappointment from your own life? I'd imagine that in the short term, that disappointment felt pretty devastating. However, I'd be willing to bet that over the long run, it served as a great learning experience.

For example, maybe it taught you not to expect that everything in life will be handed to you. Or, maybe it pushed you to train harder the following year to achieve a different goal. And maybe, both of those lessons led you to even greater outcomes. This is what I mean when I say disappointment can lead to personal growth. Without the occasional letdown, we don't get the push we need to improve ourselves and better our craft.

Many of the stories I've told in this book follow the same pattern. The crippling anxiety I felt before planning to go skydiving was an extremely difficult storm to weather. But without that experience, I wouldn't have begun to figure out what works and what doesn't when it comes to my fears and mental rehearsal. Putting ourselves in situations like these fast tracks our growth, helping us learn and change in ways that aren't possible when watching from the sidelines.

In his standout work, *Stumbling on Happiness*, psychologist Daniel Gilbert mirrors this kind of thinking. He points out how studies show that men and women who've faced major traumas end up faring quite well in the long run. According to Gilbert, it's only when the chips are down that we can discover how strong we are.[29] When placed in

---

[29] Gilbert, Daniel. "Paradise Glossed." *Stumbling on Happiness*, Vintage Books, 2005, pp. 167, 192.

these situations, we figure out how to battle through them in ways we couldn't have otherwise imagined.

Every experience can teach us something. The only meaning anything has is the one we assign to it. When we look at anxiety and disappointment myopically, it's often difficult to see the purpose of them. But when we zoom out and see how they can teach us and fuel our growth, we learn to view them in a better light.

That's not to say growth is easy or glamorous, nor that actual trauma is something we should go looking for. It's just that the challenging moments in our lives often make us stronger in the end. If we realize this, we can learn to lean into anxiety-provoking situations more readily and find purpose in traumatic experiences when they do make their way into our lives.

In the field of psychology, the personal development these painful lessons often precipitate is called *post-traumatic growth*,[30] and it's one of the very reasons I wrote this book. Ten years ago, I would've told you anxiety was the worst thing that ever happened to me. However, if you ask me about it today, I'd tell you it's been a phenomenal catalyst for my own development. That's not to say it's been easy. Little worth pursuing in life ever is. But that's the whole point. Every failure calls you to become something greater. Every disappointment beckons you to grow closer to the person you ultimately wish to be. Even though difficult, we should answer that call.

THE LINK BETWEEN PAIN AND GROWTH

Anxiety, disappointment, failure, and challenge all have one thing in common – pain. When we don't achieve what we've set out to achieve, when we lose something valuable, or miss an opportunity, it's not uncommon to feel downright awful. Pain is the ultimate survival tool for the

---

[30] Neimeyer, Robert A. "Fostering Posttraumatic Growth: A Narrative Elaboration." *Psychological Inquiry*, vol. 15, no. 1, 2004, pp. 53–59. *JSTOR*, JSTOR, www.jstor.org/stable/20447202.

human brain. It's a harbinger of danger, even death, and pushes us to move away from it.

While this tactic has promoted our survival throughout history, it's a bit of a paradox. For pain doesn't just lead to death – it also leads to growth. Determining the difference between survival-threatening pain and growth-promoting pain, then, is of the utmost importance, since it helps us figure out when to push forward versus when to turn away.

When we make this distinction and lean into the good kind of pain, we can overcome the paradox and prepare ourselves for growth. In their bestselling book, *The Telomere Effect*, Dr. Elizabeth Blackburn and Dr. Elissa Epel echo this sentiment, explaining that we can choose to see stress as either a threat or a challenge. When we choose the latter, we often open ourselves up to more energy, focus, and growth.[31]

Let's say there's an opening at your company for your dream job in a different department from where you currently work. You want to apply but are worried you'll get turned down or management will think you're not committed to your current role. Regardless of the outcome, if you push through these uneasy feelings, you'll undoubtedly experience some form of personal growth.

For example, learning to deal with your uneasy feelings over the opportunity could help you become more assertive or willing to put yourself out there in the future. Taking this risk could also give you a chance to see just what kind of candidate management is looking for. That knowledge could lead you to take up new courses and learn new things in hopes of becoming that person.

Whether you get the role or not is not actually the most important part of this situation. Learning, and growing into the person required for that role, is. That way, whenever the right opportunity presents itself, you'll be ready. If you never try or put yourself out there, you'll never

---

[31] Blackburn, Elizabeth, and Elissa Epel. "Unraveling: How Stress Gets into Your Cells." *The Telomere Effect*, Grand Central Publishing, 2017, pp. 80–91.

know what could happen or who you could become. Instead of letting your fear drive your decisions in this situation, attach to the idea of getting that dream job and let it do the talking.

While we may not realize it, many of us expose ourselves to growth-promoting pain on a daily basis. At the gym, we lift weights or engage in strenuous cardiovascular activity in order to build physical strength. We push ourselves through the pain of tough workouts so our muscles will become more powerful. We expose ourselves to soreness and exhaustion because we know strength and conditioning lie on the other side. If we applied this concept to emotional and psychological growth more often, we'd jump on a rocket ship of personal development.

Doing so is not easy, however. The only way to rationally subject ourselves to emotional and psychological pain is to rewire ourselves into believing growth and pain are inexorably intertwined. Though this is easier said than done, one way we can begin this process is by connecting to the journeys of some of the most respected figures in history and how the pain they endured on those journeys helped shape them into the philanthropic people they would ultimately become.

Think about folks like Oprah Winfrey and Victor Frankl. Winfrey was sexually abused as a child by various members of her family, while Frankl watched most of his family perish in Nazi concentration camps during World War II. Yet, despite the enormous amount of pain each of these icons experienced, both of them went on to leave massive legacies. Winfrey became one of the greatest philanthropists in American history, while Frankl wrote *Man's Search For Meaning*, one of the most influential books of all time.

I know what I've been through is beyond minuscule compared to what both Winfrey and Frankl encountered, but both stories serve as constant reminders of the link between pain and personal growth. On days when I'm struggling, I recall their stories and reconnect to the idea that there's a larger purpose to the pain I sometimes experience.

So often, we see pain and immediately hide from it. We dread putting ourselves out there because we fear failure is permanent or means we aren't good enough. Though these are valid concerns, they simply aren't true. In her best-selling book, *Mindset: The New Psychology of Growth*, professor Carol Dweck describes where these fears come from and how we can put them to rest.

Dweck's research is founded upon two opposing dispositions that, she says, many humans adopt – the fixed mindset and the growth mindset.[32] The former, Dweck details, builds its foundation on the belief that our abilities are set and we can't do anything to change them. This mindset allows little room for improvement. People adopting this mentality fail at a task and tell themselves, "I'm just no good at this, I shouldn't even try."

The growth mindset, on the other hand, comes with the belief that everything we experience gives us feedback on how we're doing. If we fail at something, this mindset dictates, it's only a sign we need to pay more attention or try harder next time. Those adopting the growth mindset, Dweck states, more readily integrate lessons provided by past failures and try again. They may know embarrassment can hurt in the moment, but they also know it can reveal to them skills required for improving and avoiding embarrassment in the future.

As corny as it sounds, bolstering our standing in life is all about learning from failure, dusting ourselves off, and getting back up again. My message here is not to make anxiety, growth, and pain seem trivial. In reality, they are messy and difficult. My only intent is to help you see them from a different perspective.

Most of us view anxiety, pain, and failure as purely negative things, which only pushes us to avoid them. But these very things from which we often run are, in reality, also the things that can accelerate our personal growth and push us into becoming the people we've always wanted to

---

[32] Dweck, Carol S. "Inside the Mindsets." *Mindset: The New Psychology of Success*, Ballantine Books, 2007, pp. 15–55.

be. As we prioritize our need for that growth, we'll move closer to our ideal selves even faster.

WE DETERMINE WHAT ANXIETY MEANS

It was springtime of my senior year of high school. I'd been seeing Monica, one of the girls I mentioned at the beginning of this book. I was pretty crazy about her. The only problem was, it didn't seem like she was that crazy about me. We'd gone on a few dates but then things cooled off a bit. I talked to her in school most days, but when it came to hanging out again, she was noncommittal. It seemed like every weekend she was out of town. When I finally got her to agree to go out with me again, I was nervous. I wondered why she'd been so distant.

The next weekend, we went out for dinner, then ended up at my parents' house. For a while, we watched TV and made harmless conversation. But, the longer we sat there, the more I wanted to ask her about us. As I thought about what I'd say and how she'd react, I felt quite anxious.

My head filled with thoughts about her ending it with me on the spot. My heart raced and I fell into a panic. This was the first time I'd ever experienced something so intense. I had no idea what was happening. I felt like I couldn't breathe. I kept quiet for a minute to gather myself while the television drowned out the drumline coming from my chest.

When I regained the ability to form semi-coherent sentences, I turned to Monica and asked why we hadn't been hanging out as of late. She brushed it off, so I asked again. After three tries, she told me she'd been seeing someone out-of-state, that it was getting serious, and that we probably shouldn't see each other anymore. It was a tough blow.

While I sat there in disbelief, she noticed how fast my heart was beating. "I can feel a pulse coming from your shirt. Are you freaking out?" I told her I wasn't, but in reality, I was. Big time. I was going through my first panic attack and break-up at the same time. I had no idea how to handle either. As I came to grips with the situation, I decided it was time to take her home. We chatted briefly in her driveway and agreed there would be no more dates. What a humbling night that was.

At the time, I didn't know much about nervousness and anxiety. In fact, I didn't even know the term *panic attack*, so it was hard for me to google my way to a diagnosis, let alone a solution. Without answers, I spent the next several weeks wondering what I had just experienced. I asked myself how I'd be able to get close to someone again, knowing this could happen at any moment. I wondered what kind of woman would tolerate their guy's heart flying out of his chest every time they hung out.

Fast-forward about one month. I was at my friend Todd's house with a bunch of the guys. One of my friends, Paul, couldn't stop talking about Mary, the girl he was seeing. He told us about a party they'd gone to a few weeks prior where they kissed for the first time. Paul recalled Mary pulling him into an empty room, where they got close. In that room, Paul noticed his heart racing. Mary noticed too. Somewhat taken aback, Mary exclaimed, "Oh my god, Paul, why is your heart beating so fast?" In a moment of uncertainty and excitement, Paul responded slyly, "Because you're so freaking hot." Then, he landed his first kiss on her.

As Paul recounted his story, something clicked in my head. "I guess I'm not the only one who's experienced a racing heartbeat in an intense situation with a pretty girl," I thought to myself. That alone was eye-opening to the eighteen-year-old me. That night, I couldn't help but wonder, "If Paul and I experienced the same physical symptoms, why is it I lost my mind while he stayed calm enough to get the girl?" I didn't have an answer at that very moment, but I had a lead, and knew I was onto something.

"WHAT DOES THIS MEAN?"

We're always trying to make sense of what's going on around us. First we gather sensory data from our environment, then we determine what that information means, then we decide whether or not to take action in response to that meaning. Sometimes, like when we instinctively slam on our breaks in bumper-to-bumper traffic, this process occurs within a fraction of a second. Other times, like when we're solving complex math problems, it takes a bit longer.

No matter what situation we find ourselves in, we're always asking ourselves, "What does this mean?" even if only subconsciously. It's only through attaching meaning to external stimuli that we can figure out what to do in response to them. Even though this process of determining meaning may at first seem like one that's out of our control, we actually have quite a bit more influence over it than you might otherwise imagine.

Take my date with Monica for example. I may not have had much control over the initial intensification of my heartbeat, but I did have control over how I reacted to it. When I looked at that heartbeat and said, "I don't know what this means, I'm scared," I subconsciously told my brain, "You are correct to turn on the overdrive system. There's something threatening happening and we must be ready for it."

That threat only seemed more and more real as my fear and anxious symptoms intensified. This cycle of intensification continued until it reached its pinnacle and I experienced what I'd describe as total overwhelm – a panic attack. Thus, my initial determination of what that fast heartbeat meant, or lack thereof, eventually became my end experience.

My friend Paul, on the other hand, found himself in a similar situation, yet looked at it in a completely different fashion. Instead of seeing his racing heart as a reason to be fearful, he took it as a sign of exhilaration and passion. He saw the pretty girl in front of him and said to himself, "This means I'm about to do something slightly risky, yet exciting. This is a really great moment." Whether he knew it or not, Paul was engaging in *anxiety reappraisal*, a strategy proven

145

by research studies to boost both mood and performance in stressful situations.[33] Such a strategy can be vital in our own anxiety journeys as well.

Sure, you could argue Paul was able to look at his situation differently because it *was* different – his relationship was starting while mine was ending. However, neither of us knew that at the time. All we knew was we needed to make sense of our racing hearts. How each of us did that supplied the reason for the vast difference in our experiences.

There's no right or wrong answer to the question of "What does this mean?" There's only the answer we provide. Whatever we tell ourselves something means, as long as we actually believe it, is what it truly means to us. Since our internal reactions are the first suppliers of meaning to our conscious and subconscious minds, it's often those reactions that most strongly influence, and later *become*, our experience.

When you really stop and think about it, a racing heartbeat during an anxious situation is not inherently negative. When we go running or ride a roller coaster, we often experience the same exact thing. The only difference between an accelerated heart rate on a thrill ride and one during an interview is how we choose to view that heart rate. With the right tools, we can change our perspectives. We can come to see our racing hearts, or any of our other anxious symptoms, as indications that something exciting is right around the corner.

THE WORDS WE USE

One of the most powerful tools we can leverage in order to change how we experience the everyday events of our lives is the language we use to describe said events. Whether we're speaking aloud or just thinking to ourselves, the specific words we use have a tremendous impact on how

---

[33] Brooks, Alison W. "Get Excited: Reappraising Pre-Performance Anxiety as Excitement." *Journal of Experimental Psychology: General*, vol. 3, June 2014, pp. 1144–1158., doi:10.1037/a0035325.

we react to, and ultimately come to view, the situation, event, or happenstance playing out in front of us.

Even though we don't always dictate our reactions, we're always speaking to ourselves internally. The process of thinking and perceiving is nothing more than seeing things unfold in front of us and making sense of them by talking to ourselves on the inside. When you walk downstairs and smell the apple pie in the oven, you might not always proclaim, "Wow, that smells amazing!" but you almost always think it.

When we describe our anxious symptoms with fearful language, our bodies react to that language and create more tension and fear within us. Thus, if the words we use to describe our experiences become our experiences, then in rethinking what words we use most often, we can theoretically reshape how we experience the events, situations, and happenings of our lives.

Think about some of the words you typically associate with anxiety. For several years after my challenging experience with Monica, most of the language I used to describe my heart palpitations, sweaty palms, and poor concentration was extremely negative. Whenever I thought about or experienced these symptoms, I described them with words like panic, dread, and doom, telling my body how it should feel in regard to them.

More often than not, this would set off a vicious cycle of reactions inside me, driving me further into anxiousness. I'd perceive sweaty palms as something negative and describe them with pessimistic self-talk, prompting my body to ready the war cannons. Then, in a heightened state, I'd describe my body's subsequent reactions with an even greater expression of fear. This cycle would often repeat until whatever elicited my initial response became a true manifestation of panic, dread, or doom.

These chain reactions inside our minds and bodies are one of the main ways anxiety comes to fruition. That's why it's imperative that you pay close attention to the words you use, both internally and externally, to describe how the events of your life unfold. Many of the things that happen in our lives are neutral by nature. It's only when we label those things with internal chatter or external dialogue that we begin to see them as either positive or negative. By moving from describing our anxious symptoms in negative fashion to neutral or positive fashion, we can alter the way we experience anxiety in real time. In order to make this concept more clear, let's look into a hypothetical example.

For a moment, let's imagine you're heading to a party for an old friend from work and are feeling a bit anxious about it. When you think about all the conversations you'll have to strike up with former coworkers, you feel dreadful and notice your palms sweating. You wonder why this feeling is coming over you. You start questioning your ability to engage in small talk and wonder if you should make other plans.

Remembering all the strategies we've discussed thus far, you quickly snap back to reality and resolve to cut off your negative self-talk as quickly as you can. You recall that attaching pessimistic language to your anxious symptoms will only make them worse. You tell yourself parties with old friends are always going to be slightly daunting because you have no idea what will happen during them. However, just because you're feeling tense at the moment doesn't mean the party will go horrifically.

Now that you've begun to turn the self-talk train around, you realize your body is just preparing to do something it hasn't done in a while. You know uncertainty lies at the heart of anxiety and see the uncertainty in this situation as you not having convinced yourself that all your conversations will go swimmingly. Luckily, you know such feelings of uncertainty are par for the course in this scenario. Recalling this fact helps you ward off these feelings, which prevents them from dragging you down further.

Next, you remember the story about my friend Paul and wonder if you might be able to turn the fearful energy you're feeling into positive energy. You recall that the lens through which you view your feelings often dictates whether they intensify or not. As such, you ask yourself if maybe this energy is preparing you to be excited and fully engaged in your conversations at the party. What a great thing that would be.

There's no need to rush things, however. You decide maybe you're not quite ready to turn your fear into positive energy just yet. Simply getting through the party will do for now. You stick that strategy in your back pocket for later, however. Feeling like your new perspectives are enough to get you to the outing, you grab your keys and hit the road. You enjoy all the conversations you have, and don't realize until you get home that once you dove head first into catching up with your old friends, you didn't think about your anxiety again.

Now of course, this party example is just one illustration of how you could work through your fear and use self-talk to cut your anxiety and negativity off at the source. There are countless other examples as well as thousands of words you could use to reframe your experience and turn your fear around as soon as it rears its ugly head.

When you stop using fear-based words to describe the experiences you most commonly associate with anxiety, or even remove words like panic and doom from your vocabulary entirely, you'll experience those feelings less often. When you label your debilitating symptoms with more empowering words and phrases, you'll experience those symptoms in a much less debilitating way. That's why it's so important to pay attention to the words you're using to describe your everyday experiences.

As you take up these sorts of practices, it's also important to count your wins as they occur. After coming out on the other side of a challenging situation, pat yourself on the back for having pushed yourself into your fear. Doing so, will, over time, help drown out the negativity in your mind that makes you feel like every fear-inducing situation will end horrifically. This will, in turn, make you even more likely to push yourself into similar situations in the future.

These tactics might seem like a bunch of mumbo jumbo or feel-good nonsense, but they're actually the basis of a widely accepted form of psychotherapy – Cognitive Behavioral Therapy.[34] Through changing our thoughts, attitudes, and behaviors, CBT aims to alter how we ultimately view the different events and happenings of our lives. As you start to use more empowering words to describe your fears, you'll utilize some of the basic premises of CBT. Hopefully, as you leverage those premises more and more, you'll eventually see that fear in a whole new light.

34 Field, Thomas A, et al. "The New ABCs: A Practitioner's Guide to Neuroscience-Informed Cognitive-Behavior Therapy." *Journal of Mental Health Counseling*, vol. 37, no. 3, July 2015, pp. 206–220., doi:10.17744/1040-2861-37.3.206.

CARE LESS, OPEN MORE

Keeping a cool head in the middle of a meltdown is not an easy thing to do. When feelings of doubt and fear flood our minds, it's often difficult to remember that these feelings don't always mean something's wrong. One of the main reasons we have difficulty tuning these feelings out is that we care too much about them.

We care what other people think of us and how we'll look if we're visibly fearful in front of them. On some level, we feel we shouldn't have to experience these feelings. As such, we often resist them. Yet even in our resistance, we find that our symptoms typically only get worse. As bizarre as it may sound, in order to overcome these symptoms, we need to learn to stop caring about them so much. We need to learn to stop resisting them so they can pass through us faster.

I want you to think back to grade school for a moment. Can you remember the biggest bully in your class and the kids he or she picked on? In my class, the kids who got picked on typically had something different about them, be it a lisp or an atypical haircut. Whatever it was, my class bully quickly found these differences and ridiculed my classmates for them.

He'd pick on these kids by saying things like, "Hey, nice haircut, loser! Did your mom give you that?" Feeling criticized, his victims almost always responded in defensive fashion. "Stop picking on me! It is not a weird haircut!" Yet, no matter how hard these kids fought back, the class bully would only come back with even more vengeance.

Every once in a while, this bully would find a new target. And even once in a greater while, he'd find something he never expected: some kids fighting back in a different fashion. Instead of lashing out at their foe and demanding he stop, they'd pay him no attention whatsoever.

The first time I saw a classmate of mine do this, I was stunned. I mean what could be more counterintuitive than someone making fun of your style or family and not doing anything about it? It almost seemed cowardly. But the more I thought about it, the more I realized this wasn't cowardly behavior at all. It was a sign my classmate didn't care what the bully had to say. He knew the bully's words didn't define who he was. Over time, the bully stopped picking on him and found a new victim.

I know this example seems somewhat unrelated to the topic at hand, but there's an important underlying concept we can learn from it. That concept is the fact that, similarly to how our classroom bullies stopped picking on their nonreactive classmates, our anxious symptoms often retreat when we stop fighting them.

Even though it may seem like a worthwhile effort to lash out against our fears, the energy and emotion we spend lashing out only serve to show the things affecting us that they have power over us. If we really didn't care, we wouldn't do anything or react at all. And when we don't do anything at all, our bullies and our anxious symptoms often find themselves powerless and move on.

You've probably heard it before, but it's true in so many areas of our lives: *what we resist persists*. When we say to ourselves, "Go away, heart palpitations, I won't tolerate you being here!" we don't make them go away any faster. Instead, we actually cause them to stick around longer than they'd originally planned. This is because showing our symptoms we care usually means reacting with more tension and fear, both of which make it harder for our bodies to return to equilibrium quickly.

One of the most straightforward ways we can learn to care less about experiencing anxiety is by understanding just how commonplace it is. Please don't get me wrong, when I say commonplace, I in no way mean trivial. I think we all understand how difficult anxiety can be to deal with. I just mean that if you look at the statistics, you'll likely find that what you're going through is something so many of us go through as well.

According to *The Anxiety and Depression Association of America*, 18.1% of adults aged eighteen years and older in the United States suffer from some form of anxiety disorder.[35] Moreover, 31.2% of American adults battle at least one form of anxiety at some point in their lives.[36] In reality, these numbers are likely even higher than stated. Without question, there are folks out there that have yet to report their condition or seek treatment.

One of the main reasons we resist our anxious feelings and symptoms is that we think they're abnormal or that we shouldn't be experiencing them. We weave in and out of fear-coated days and think to ourselves, "What is wrong with me?" I've asked myself this question before and, much like looping-thinking, it doesn't lead anywhere good.

Nothing is wrong with you. There's nothing to be ashamed of or embarrassed about when it comes to mental health. We all go through hardships from time to time. We almost all get nervous once in a while. We just rarely express our true feelings, which sometimes leads us to believe we're the only ones suffering. As the data shows, such is not the case.

Anxiety and survival are closely related. If we didn't feel fearful on occasion, we'd either be dead or our ancestors wouldn't have lived long enough for us to be here. The mere fact that you can sense your pain means you're self-aware. That's a beautiful thing. For once you stop looking at that pain as abnormal, you can finally start using it to guide you where you want to go in life. Looking at your mental health struggles as abnormal only causes them to proliferate. When you step back and say, "I'm not the only person who experiences this," you learn to fight your anxiety less, which in turn, helps you use it instead of letting it use you.

---

[35] "Facts & Statistics." *Anxiety and Depression Association of America*, adaa.org/about-adaa/press-room/facts-statistics.
[36] Beidel, Deborah C, et al. "Anxiety, Trauma, and Stressor-Related Disorders." *Abnormal Psychology: A Scientist-Practitioner Approach*, 4th ed., Pearson Education, Inc., 2017, pp. 121.

There's no denying that depression, doubt, fear, and anxious symptoms are very real and difficult things to get through. Yet, just because these things are difficult doesn't mean we should let them control us, nor should we ignore the basic principles of how they work. For years, I did these very things. I spent most of my waking hours fighting my anxiety, trying to show it I wouldn't back down. I did this because I cared. I cared about having a panic attack in public. I cared about feeling vulnerable or abnormal. I cared about looking like a tough guy. It wasn't until I realized I needed to stop caring so much about my anxiety that I finally made some progress with it.

As much as we hate to admit it, most of us really do care too much about our conditions. And so, like our schoolmates who got picked on in class, we push back against our fears because we don't want to appear vulnerable, not realizing that in our push back, we expose our vulnerability and open ourselves up to even greater levels of distress. When we finally start caring less, we'll begin making some serious progress with our demons.

CANDOR: A PARADOXICAL SOLUTION

While we're on the subject of caring less about our anxiety and the paradoxical effect it often has, I'd be remiss if I didn't also bring up the quality of candor – the characteristic of being open and honest with ourselves and others.

I'm sure you've met someone who embodies this trait. He's the guy on the city bus who recites his entire life story before you even have a chance to put in your headphones. One minute he's stepping onto the bus, and the next, he's telling you about his sister who's a degenerate gambler, his brother who's addicted to pills, and his dog who's a recovering alcoholic. Joking aside, it's obvious these kinds of people have one thing in common: they give zero shits. Though not caring in life obviously comes with its own host of problems, there's something we can learn from these folks – the power of candor.

Candor is so powerful because it shows an overall comfortability with one's character, which is the exact opposite of the uptightness that often comes with an anxious personality. When we feel that uptightness, we often rush to contain it. We push our anxiety down, praying it will go away in high pressure situations. We tell other people we're fine even when we're on the brink of a panic attack.

Even though these defensive tactics seem logical, they don't help us curb our anxiety because they're just different forms of resistance. As we've discussed, when we resist our anxiety, it paradoxically fights us back even harder. When we hold that anxiety in and refuse to discuss it with anyone, we cause our symptoms to fester and wreak havoc within our minds.

The way out of this paradox is the way of candor. By opening up about our symptoms, by telling ourselves and others what's going on, we subconsciously let our minds know that what we're feeling is okay, even if it's frightening. Telling ourselves things are okay helps the body feel safer, faster. And once the body feels safe, it typically powers down the emergency alert systems shortly thereafter.

To drive this point home, let's pretend you're auditioning for a singing contest and are having a bit of a nervous breakdown on stage. Instead of trying to fight through the anxiety in the moment, you could turn to the judges and say something like, "I'm really sorry. I'm just feeling a bit nervous right now because this is such an important day for me." Though it might sound like self-sabotage, such an admission could prove beneficial. Here's why.

Most people love honesty. Having seen countless auditions before, the judges know anxiety comes with the territory. Even though you might think that showing your vulnerability would make them boo you off stage, my guess is the opposite would be more likely to happen. That is, the judges would likely connect to similar fears they once had and root for the part of themselves they see in you.

Your candor might be more beneficial than that as well. By being open and honest with the judges, it's possible your in-the-moment fear would retreat too. For many of us who experience anxiety, there's a fear we'll be found out, exposed as anxious and nervous people. When we expose ourselves intentionally, we short-circuit our anxiety. We take control of the situation by telling our symptoms they aren't such a big deal. When we do this, we no longer have to fear being exposed – we've done that ourselves already. This signals our fight-or-flight systems to ramp down for the time being.

Even though you may never find yourself in the midst of a singing competition, I think you'll find that being honest about your symptoms leads you down a similar path in almost any situation. That is, your frankness can help you connect with others and make them want to provide a helping hand. When we hold our anxiety inside, we act nervously, yet pretend everything's okay, leaving people thinking we're strange or awkward. Though stepping out and talking about our fears doesn't exactly seem like a logical way to mitigate them, most of anxiety is a paradox. And when we're dealing with paradoxes, the most obvious answers aren't always the right ones.

Candor is also paramount in helping us overcome the kind of anxiety that lives at a higher level, outside of any one specific event or situation. Take flying for example. A few of my friends are so anxious about it that they wouldn't even get on a plane for an all-expenses-paid, paradise vacation – a mere conversation about planes is a nightmare for these folks. Even though it might sound terrifying to them, I think opening up about their fears would do these friends a world of good. To show you what I mean, let's pretend you're one of these people.

One day you're feeling a bit more open about your aviation apprehension than usual. You start small and decide to do some research on the subject. Even though you fear finding information or statistics that could leave you more afraid of flying, you think to yourself, "I'm not getting on a plane today regardless, so why would that change anything?"

As you start your search, you quickly come across a journal article revealing that in 1982, one in six Americans was afraid of flying commercially.[37] With how quickly negative stories travel in today's age of digital media, including those pertaining to aviation, you imagine that number probably hasn't changed much since. And if it hasn't, then maybe, you tell yourself, you have nothing to be ashamed of in being scared of flying.

That realization leads you to be even more open and honest about your fears. The next day, while discussing travel plans at the office, you take a bigger step and confide your fear to one of your coworkers. In return, she describes how she used to be deathly afraid of flying as well. Once she did some research of her own, however, she felt there wasn't all that much to be afraid of. After all, she tells you, you're more likely to die in a fire or while driving to work than you are on a commercial airliner.[38]

All of this information makes you feel pretty good. So good, in fact, that you spend your night researching everything that makes planes safe. You read about how planes are equipped to deal with mechanical failures, power outages, inclement weather, and the like. You learn terms like lift, drag, and thrust, and come to realize that getting a plane in the sky is more physics than it is magic. And while all of that information doesn't get you on the next flight out, it certainly helps you entertain the possibility of flying much more seriously.

Without opening yourself up, without being willingly vulnerable about your fear, it's likely you would've never allowed yourself the opportunity to find the assuring information and statistics that you did. That's true of anxiety in general as well. When we hold our fears inside and worry they'll come true, they eat away at us. Yet, when we're courageous enough to talk about them, we find we not only lessen those fears by resisting them less, but we also open ourselves up to more support, more information, and better ways to deal with those fears.

---

[37] Dean, Robert D, and Kerry M Whitaker. "Fear of Flying: Impact on the US Air Travel Industry." *Journal of Travel Research*, vol. 21, no. 1, 1 July 1982, pp. 7–17., doi:10.1177/004728758202100104.
[38] "What Are the Odds of Dying From.." *National Safety Council*, 2017, www.nsc.org/work-safety/tools-resources/injury-facts/chart.

A DISCIPLINED MIND

I introduced, early in this book, the idea that our thoughts influence how we feel on both a short-term and long-term basis. Each thought we have carries with it an electrical impulse. The longer and more intensely we focus on a specific thought, the stronger the accompanying electrical impulse becomes, and thus, the more it affects us.

What this means in practice is if we focus on negative thoughts for long periods of time, we're going to feel stressed out and anxious. Conversely, if we think positive thoughts for extended durations, we'll likely avoid stress and might even feel joyous or carefree. And we all want to feel joyous, so we'll all just think good thoughts for the rest of time, right? Not exactly. I'll explain.

We often think and attach to negative thoughts, even when we know their effect on us, because our brains, whether we like it or not, are attracted to negative things. I don't mean that in the sense that we enjoy negative things. I'm simply referring to the fact that our brains see all negative thoughts, stimuli, and possibilities as threats to our survival. Since our brains are wired for survival, they often react to those thoughts as if there truly were something life-threatening in front of us, even when there isn't.

When our bodies are on high alert due to stress, we often feel like we need to do something to counteract that stress, regardless of whether that's actually the case. Since there's rarely a fierce predator in front of us to run away from, we can't always dispel the energy that comes with a fight-or-flight reaction easily. Without an obvious escape plan, we often use that fear in disempowering ways.

We think faster and deeper, typically in negative fashion, about the symptoms we're experiencing or the thoughts that spurred our reaction in the first place. Even when we know we should give no attention to these negative thoughts, our bodies often trick us and suck us into them.

In order for us to get better at resisting the urge to give in to these negative thoughts, we must develop what's called *a disciplined mind* – a term I've borrowed from The Dalai Lama and his impactful book, *The Art of Happiness*.[39] In his work, The Dalai Lama describes the same sentiment I just recapped: thoughts are things and if we want to feel good, we need to practice thinking good thoughts and blocking out negative ones more often. A disciplined mind then, as The Dalai Lama describes, is a mind that pays careful attention to the quality of its thoughts and only lets in those that will lead to good feelings or productive behaviors.

MEDITATION

Though being mindful in our everyday lives is a good way to start developing mental discipline, I don't think it's totally sufficient. Without taking a more direct approach, we run the risk of having the lower, survival-based parts of our brains hijack our analytical and rational capacities again and again.

What we need then, is an active strategy we can apply consistently in order to expand our thought-filtering skills. Think of such a strategy as the mental form of lifting weights to build stronger muscles. The only difference is, through this technique, we'll be developing stronger thought-filtering capacities. This strategy is the ancient art of meditation.

The word meditation describes a practice in which a person focuses his or her mind on a specific thought or object in order to gain mental clarity or enter a desirable emotional state. This practice is thought to have its roots in Hinduism and ancient Indian culture,[40] and, according to

---

[39] The Dalai Lama and Howard C Cutler. "Training the Mind for Happiness." *The Art of Happiness*, Riverhead Books, 1998, pp. 37–51.
[40] Sharma, Hari. "Meditation: Process and Effects." *AYU*, vol. 36, no. 3, 2015, pp. 233–237., doi:10.4103/0974-8520.182756.

historians, traces back to as early as 1500 BCE.[41] Though meditation originally gained popularity as a religious ritual, today, many of us know it for its stress-relieving capabilities.

The practice of meditation is simple, albeit not easy. The goal is to focus on a specific thought or object intently in order to lower the speed and stress of your conscious mind. In order to get started, you'll need to decide what you're going to focus on during your session. We'll call that thing your *meditational focus*. There are no hard and fast rules when it comes to choosing a meditational focus. All that matters is it's something positive that can be defined in just a few words or sounds.

The reason your focus should be simple is that the goal of meditation is not to get lost in the specifics of the *how*, but to focus on the *what* while letting everything else in your mind drift away. Your focus need not be an outcome you want to make happen either. You can also focus on your breathing, a specific word or sound, or a mantra. Just choose something specific enough that it won't send you down the path of overthinking or questioning during your session.

Once you've decided upon a meditational focus, find a place you can sit comfortably with minimal distraction. Unlike what you may see on television or the internet, you don't need a dedicated room of the house for meditation, nor do you need any trendy workout gear or fancy equipment. That's the best part. You can meditate pretty much anywhere, so long as it's a place you can sit upright and shut out what's going on around you.

Once seated, close your eyes and begin breathing slowly and deeply through your diaphragm. You'll know you're doing this correctly when your belly rises and falls instead of your chest. Then, while breathing slowly and deeply, place your mind's eye on your meditational focus. This is your only task while meditating. Though it might

---

[41] Everly, George S, and Jeffrey M Lating. "Meditation." *A Clinical Guide to the Treatment of the Human Stress Response*, 1st ed., Springer, 1989, p. 171.

sound like both a breeze and a bore at the same time, in practice, it's actually quite challenging. This is why I say meditation is simple but not easy; you don't actually have to do all that much, and that's what makes it difficult.

Our jobs and phones train us to be *on* all the time. Our minds often race endlessly, and it can be very difficult to turn them off. As you meditate, you'll find that your racing mind often prohibits you from successfully staying locked on your meditational focus. Thoughts you weren't expecting will come out of nowhere and ask you to give them attention. This is the most difficult thing about meditation and it's extremely common to experience.

When these thoughts make their way into your mind, try to look at them without reacting to them. Send them on their way, then return your mind's eye to your meditational focus. Just because a thought enters your mind doesn't mean you need to give it any attention. This concept applies regardless of whether you're meditating or not. When random, scary ideas pop into your head, rather than focus on them and send yourself down the rabbit hole, try to let them go.

Sure, sometimes it feels like the universe is sending us these thoughts for a reason. While I'm sure that could happen, most of the time, I'd say that's not the case. I've always told myself that random thoughts pop up because our brains are constantly reorganizing ideas and memories. Sometimes, as a side effect of that process, I wager, said thoughts fall into our conscious minds.

While I don't have scientific evidence of that claim, it has helped me not worry so much about these kinds of thoughts. I've wrestled with these monsters countless times before. I'm sure you have too. I can assure you, doing so only leads to misery. Do yourself a favor and drop them when they arise. The more you meditate, the better you'll get at doing so.

Don't fret if all of this doesn't come easily at first or even after several sessions. I've been meditating for years and I still struggle with my focus from time to time. That's just how our minds work. The key to being successful with meditation is to not beat yourself up when you do find your mind wandering. Doing so will only create tension in your body and make it harder for you to get back to your focus.

Continue this practice for about five minutes at first and see how you do. As you get better with it, you can increase the length and frequency of your sessions. I recommend five-minute sessions for a week to start.

In the short-term, meditation is all about leveraging a specific focus to turn off the seemingly incessant flow of negative or looping thoughts in our minds. In the long-term, the goal of meditation is to develop the disciplined mind The Dalai Lama prescribes. That mind is one that's less reactive, in general, to negative thoughts, and more attuned to the benefits that positive and uplifting thoughts have on our well-being. It takes time and dedication, but if you stick with it, you'll eventually develop a more resilient psyche you can call upon at will to get out of almost any challenging emotional state.

TREATING YOUR BODY RIGHT

Much of our discussion thus far has centered around the various ways we can use our minds to lower our internal reactions in situations where anxiety comes knocking. One area we have yet to discuss in regard to that anxiety is that of treating our bodies in a way that leads to less pain and stress overall. In this chapter, we'll go in-depth on how putting the right things in our bodies and getting the proper amount of sleep can give us a leg up against fear.

FOOD AND WATER

The foods we eat and the amount of water we consume have a large effect on our day-to-day experience of anxiety. Eating the right foods and drinking enough water helps us feel good physically, which in turn, allows us to dedicate more energy and attention to the things that help us feel good mentally, such as blocking out negative thoughts and focusing on good ones.

Think back to the last time you had a stomach ache. When your body hurt physically, wasn't it so much harder to keep a positive frame of mind? I know that's the case when I don't feel well. When our bodies are sick or in pain, we spend much of our mental capacities reacting to our feelings and symptoms. And when we use our cerebral resources to monitor our bodies, we often let our guard down elsewhere, allowing anxiety-provoking thoughts to enter our minds.

The claim that eating the wrong foods can leave us feeling stressed out is one that has its basis in both biology and scientific research. Digestion is one of the most taxing exercises our bodies perform. When we fill our stomachs with harmful foods or ones that are hard to break down, we force our bodies to expend a great deal of energy processing and digesting those foods. We also make ourselves susceptible to upset stomachs, nausea, diarrhea, and a whole host of other yucky symptoms.

If you've ever experienced a *food coma*, you've witnessed this energy depletion firsthand. When we overeat, especially on the wrong foods, our bodies become overwhelmed by the chaos in our stomachs. In order to retain the energy required to break down all the food we've binged on, they turn down the dials on almost all of our other functions, leaving us feeling sluggish and foggy.

Though we all respond differently to what we put in our bodies, science suggests that heavily processed foods and animal products make us feel more distressed than just about anything else that we eat. Processed foods, including breads, pastas, donuts, muffins, fried foods, candies, soft drinks, and other sweets often contain high amounts of salt or sugar, but lack the fiber required for slowing down the digestion of these compounds. These unnatural combinations of ingredients can throw our systems out of whack and create a plethora of undesirable side effects.[42]

Take sandwich bread, for example. In nature, there are no loaves of your favorite brands hanging from trees. There are only raw and unprocessed foods such as those coming from plants. Most whole, plant-based foods provide us with fiber, which slows digestion and causes the molecules in these foods to enter our bloodstreams more gradually. The flour in white bread does not fit this pattern. It's heavily processed and devoid of the fiber found in whole wheat. As such, it gets digested and assimilated into our bloodstreams rapidly.

Since the flour in white bread is made of starches, digesting it can make us feel like we've just poured pure sugar into our veins. These starches send our blood glucose,

---

[42] Afaghi, Ahmad, et al. "High-Glycemic-Index Carbohydrate Meals Shorten Sleep Onset." *The American Journal of Clinical Nutrition*, vol. 85, no. 2, 1 Feb. 2007, pp. 426–430., doi:10.1093/ajcn/85.2.426.

or blood sugar, skyrocketing.[43] This is not the case with whole foods like lentils or apples; the fiber in these foods slows their sugar content from entering our bloodstreams so quickly.

When our blood sugar spikes, we might feel an initial boost, but the high doesn't last long. After a short-lived buzz, it often comes crashing back down below normal levels, which can leave us feeling dizzy, fatigued, or lightheaded. This is true not just for white bread but also many of the flour-based products we consume today.

Animal products are difficult for our bodies to digest as well. Calorically, they're some of the densest foods on the planet. As such, we can eat more of them before we feel full. Dr. Joel Fuhrman, the celebrity doctor and best-selling author, describes this concept in his book, *Eat To Live*.

In his work, Dr. Fuhrman states that one of the ways our bodies detect they should stop eating is through volume receptors in the stomach. According to Fuhrman, our stomachs can hold up to about one liter of food. Thus, the more calorically dense the food we eat is, the more we can jam into our stomachs before our volume receptors can tell we're full.[44]

This increased intake of calories means more difficult digestions for our bodies and more experiences of *food coma*. In addition, more food and more calories in our stomachs increases the likelihood of stomach aches and indigestion. The bottom line? If you want to feel better physically, try eating fewer processed foods and animal products.

So, if we shouldn't be eating so many processed foods and animal products, what exactly should we be eating? Just about anything else. Specifically, any whole, plant-based foods, including fruits, vegetables, grains, legumes, nuts, or seeds. These foods are not only easier for our bodies to

---

[43] Jenkins, David JA, et al. "Glycemic Index: Overview of Implications in Health and Disease." *The American Journal of Clinical Nutrition*, vol. 76, no. 1, 1 July 2002, pp. 266S–273S., doi:10.1093/ajcn/76/1.266S.
[44] Fuhrman, Joel. "Nutritional Wisdom Makes You Thin." *Eat to Live: The Amazing Nutrient-Rich Program for Fast and Sustained Weight Loss*, Little, Brown Spark, 2011, pp. 116–125.

break down, but they also come without the nasty side effect of blood sugar crashes. In addition, most of these foods are calorically light, meaning it's harder for us to overeat on them or get an upset stomach because of them.

Though I don't want to turn this into a full-blown nutrition class, there's one caveat in regard to eating new foods that I must address, and that's the fact that so many of us are addicted to the foods we eat. Processed foods and animal products, even though hazardous to our health in large amounts, often provide us with such a dopamine high that we grow accustomed to the immediate rewards of eating them.

When we try to rid ourselves of these foods, our bodies can often feel worse before they feel better. This is completely normal, Dr. Fuhrman states, and does not indicate that we're damaging our bodies. Just as smokers experience withdrawal when they give up cigarettes, we may also experience painful feelings when we give up the unhealthy foods we've eaten for so long.[45]

It can be difficult, at first, to introduce new foods into your diet because of those pesky withdrawal feelings, but if you push through your initial discomforts, you'll soon discover you don't need the foods you're addicted to so much anymore. Soon thereafter, you may even find that the new, whole foods you're eating actually make you feel quite good, physically. As you start feeling better physically, hopefully you'll find it easier to dedicate the energy required for disciplined and positive thinking.

When it comes to water, most of us aren't drinking enough. Just like how eating poorly affects how we feel physically, so too does being dehydrated. As a basic rule of thumb, try drinking about one half ounce of water for every pound that you weigh, daily. For example, if you weigh 180 pounds, aim to drink around 90 ounces every twenty-four hours.

---

[45] Fuhrman, Joel. "Your Plan For Substantial Weight Reduction." *Eat to Live: The Amazing Nutrient-Rich Program for Fast and Sustained Weight Loss*, Little, Brown Spark, 2011, pp. 233-234.

Our bodies are made of more than 50% water.[46] Our brains, even more. When we're dehydrated, our bodies and brains don't operate as smoothly or efficiently as normal. Just about all of us have experienced this phenomenon firsthand. Today, more research studies are proving what we've been feeling already: we just aren't ourselves when we're thirsty.

Take, for example, a 2015 study conducted at Loughborough University that hypothesized that being dehydrated while performing everyday tasks, such as driving, would lead to more errors in performance than being hydrated. Trials conducted in this very study seemed to not only prove this initial hypothesis, but also suggest that dehydration can be just as detrimental on task performance as a blood-alcohol level around the legal limit.[47]

When our brains aren't functioning properly due to dehydration, cognition suffers, making it much harder for us to stay focused or keep ourselves out of the looping thought patterns that lead to anxiety. For us, that's just another reason to become more self-aware and mindful. When our stomachs hurt or we're feeling tired, we need to ask ourselves how we've treated our bodies that day and make changes when necessary.

SLEEP

While we're on the subject of feeling lethargic, we must also talk about the effect sleep has on our experience of anxiety. My basic argument is a continuation of that from the previous section; it's harder for us to do the thought-work required for staying out of our heads when we don't feel well physically. Just like having a headache throws us

---

[46] "Water: How Much Should You Drink Every Day?" *Mayo Clinic*, 6 Sept. 2017, www.mayoclinic.org/healthy-lifestyle/nutrition-and-healthy-eating/in-depth/water/art-20044256.
[47] Watson, P, et al. "Mild Hypohydration Increases the Frequency of Driver Errors during a Prolonged, Monotonous Driving Task." *Physiology & Behavior*, vol. 147, 1 Aug. 2015, pp. 313–318., doi:10.1016/j.physbeh.2015.04.028.

off our game, so too does being exhausted due to lack of sleep.

We've all said it to a friend or colleague before. "I'm sorry, I'm not thinking clearly. I didn't get enough sleep last night." Whether it's editing school papers or putting together last quarter's marketing numbers, performing tasks that require critical thinking are much more difficult when we're worn out. If we want to operate at consistent, high levels, it's not enough to just be disciplined with what we put in our bodies. We also have to be disciplined with the quality and quantity of our sleep.

Like your parents and doctor always said, you should aim to get about eight hours of sleep every day. Though I typically get all of my sleep at night, I also occasionally supplement my evening sleep with a fifteen to thirty minute nap, midday, when feasible. For me, being well-rested helps me stay alert, ready to assume guard at the door of my mind.

The other reason I find sleep so important in regard to my own mental health is that it serves as a reset button on my fears. As we've discussed, anxiety gains momentum as we drive further into loops of negative or obsessive thinking. In order to lower the amount of fear we're feeling, we need to break out of these looping thoughts. Unfortunately, however, it can be very difficult to do so. All too often, our greatest fears distract us and steal our attention.

At the end of a long, worry-filled day, it's not uncommon for the momentum behind our anxious thoughts to be massive. This momentum makes it harder for us to stop flipping them over in our minds. As such, we often find ourselves trapped in our heads, ruminating on these fearful thoughts, without a way out. That's where sleep comes in. Though we obviously can't just go to sleep any time we feel anxious, we can use our evening slumber to strategically decrease the momentum of our fears.

Sleep helps take our focus off the things scaring us when little else will work. It shuts down our conscious minds, the place where so much of our anxiety lives. This not only gets us out of our heads for the night, but also provides some mental clarity the next morning.

When we wake up from a full night's sleep, we often find that the thoughts that worried us the previous day don't feel as momentous as they did when we went to bed. Sure, those thoughts are typically still there in the morning, but they usually don't feel quite the same. That's because our minds have reset and cooled off. No longer worked up from our looping-thinking, we can more rationally decline the opportunity to engage in obsessing over disappointments and doomsday scenarios. This kind of rationality can be so difficult to uncover when we're stuck in infinite fear loops.

Thankfully, there's more to the relationship between sleep and anxiety than just my quasi-scientific reasonings. Many members of the medical community have dedicated their careers to researching this unbreakable bond. Take Matthew Walker, PhD, for example. Dr. Walker is the director of the sleep and neuroimaging lab at the University of California, Berkeley, and is one of the most eminent voices in sleep research today.

In his standout book, *Why We Sleep*, Doctor Walker addresses the direct correlation between lack of sleep and anxiety, suggesting that when we get a good night's sleep, the parts of our brains involved in cognition exert a stronger control over the regions that produce fear and other powerful emotions. When we don't get enough sleep, Walker suggests, we lose this control and subject ourselves to mood swings, impulsivity, and anxiety.[48]

Walker isn't the only researcher investigating the links between sleep and mental illness. Countless other studies and research projects continue to be published each year. One of those projects, a longitudinal epidemiological study of young adults, suggests that a lack of sleep increases one's risk for developing anxiety disorders and other mental illnesses by as much as 100%.[49]

---

[48] Walker, Matthew. "Too Extreme for the Guinness Book of World Records: Sleep Deprivation and the Brain." *Why We Sleep*, Scribner, 2017, p. 147.

[49] Breslau, N, et al. "Sleep Disturbance and Psychiatric Disorders: a Longitudinal Epidemiological Study of Young Adults." *Biological*

Though it doesn't take a scientist to understand the importance of sleep on well-being, seeing research like Dr. Walker's or studies like the aforementioned certainly strengthens the argument and helps give us the leverage we need over ourselves to get our sleep schedules back on track. Without giving our bodies the rest they so desperately need, we're liable to sleepwalk through our lives, veiled by fear.

Both the common sense and the science speak loudly: sleep and mental health are intimately intertwined. If we want to lower the frequency with which we wrestle our mental demons, we seriously need to start giving ourselves the sleep we deserve. Our bodies can be a great teacher in this journey through anxiety, if we're just willing to listen to them.

Psychiatry, vol. 39, no. 6, 15 Mar. 1996, pp. 411–418., doi:10.1016/0006-3223(95)00188-3.

TAKE BACK YOUR POWER

Up to this point in the book, we've focused on explaining where anxiety comes from and what it really means. We've developed numerous in-the-moment strategies as well as lifelong habits we can leverage to counteract fear. While I believe all of these strategies are extremely effective, not all of them portray anxiety as a helpful or accepted guest. That is, many of them come off as ways to counter a negative, unwanted experience. If we truly want to move on from anxiety in the long run, we have to come to view it as something not to be feared, but welcomed.

STUCK IN PARK

In both short-term anxious situations and more prolonged ones, our survival mechanisms activate in order to keep us safe from whatever's scaring us. In acute situations, this can come in the form of accelerated heartbeats, sweaty palms, and the like. For more prolonged cases, this could instead mean increased levels of cortisol in the blood or feelings of doubt or paranoia.

In either case, our body's stress responses often make us feel like we need to do something. That is, run away from the stress or fight the threat in front of us. The only problem is, much of the time, there is no physical threat in front of us. There's only an elusive, inner demon toying with us. This confuses us to no end. We want to do something in response to the fear, but don't know what that something should be.

This confusion, combined with the energy our bodies create through the stress-response system, often makes us feel like we're going to blow. Much to our dismay, however, we typically have no way of removing this excess energy or emptying the tank. Without rechanneling this extra energy, it can wear us down or make us feel overwhelmed. When overwhelmed, we're more likely to engage in disempowering behaviors in order to feel better, such as eating sweets or drinking alcoholic beverages.

I like to use an analogy to describe this sort of internal energy overload. Think of it like being a car stuck in park. You're sitting in the driveway with the engine revving, but you're not going anywhere. You know being in high gear for too long could damage your engine, you just don't know how to get out of that revved up state.

When it comes to our own internal environments, being stuck in fifth gear might mean being stressed out or on high alert for extended periods of time. Just like incessantly revving a car can damage the engine, being strained constantly can lead to unexplained physical pains or illnesses. In order to get out of this high gear, we need to take ourselves out of park. We need to use our idling energy as fuel for physical activity or mission-driven work.

This kind of thinking is not too different from our discussions on healthy distraction – when you feel the anxious energy building inside you, you need to get up and move your body or give yourself something else to focus on. In this chapter, we'll take that logic one step further; instead of only using things like physical activity to distract us from our fears, we'll also seek to leverage that fear directly, into productivity or meaningful contribution.

Fear, like any emotion, is fuel. We can either let an excess of that fuel erode our inner temples, or we can use it to take us places. For example, when I'm feeling really anxious, I try to hit the gym or go for a run. I know I could just as easily let the fear push me into lethargy, but I'd rather channel it into an impetus for exercise. When I'm done with my workout or run, I often find I've used up most of that anxious energy. Having accomplished something with that energy is a great bonus to relieving the stress.

When I say feelings are fuel, I mean they tell us what to do. If we do things that make us feel good, our positive feelings propel us to repeat those actions. When we do things that make us feel sad or disappointed, our negative feelings push us away from repeating those very behaviors. That's why we must listen to our feelings. If we instead block or resist them, they get stuck inside us where they grow and fester. The larger they grow, the harder they become to move through and the more havoc they wreak on our mental state.

Of course, it's not always easy to listen to our feelings. It takes courage and discipline. We may not always want to hear what they're telling us. But when we do, we allow them to move through us while leveraging the energy with which they bring their message. Since anxiety is something we feel, we can listen to it too. We can face it and turn it into a force for good rather than a destructive power. This very practice is what it means to *take your power back*.

FOCUS OUTSIDE OF YOURSELF

Working out is just one approach we can take to rechannel stress when it pushes us into feeling like we need to do something. Another approach I'd like to discuss, mission-driven work, is, arguably, a more powerful application of our anxious energy. Before we talk about what mission-driven work looks like in practice, let's first discuss why it's so important.

It's no stretch to say America is the "me" country. Foreigners are often quick to label us as selfish, greedy, and superficial. It's hard to argue with those classifications. As a whole, we truly are some of the most self-interested people in the world. Yet despite how much we focus and work on ourselves, we aren't getting any happier as a nation. The explanation for this finding is simple.

We're focused on the wrong things. We care more about getting the next iPhone and sending out high-res selfies than we do finding a passionate mission in life. We care more about what other people think of us than we do ourselves. And so we go, working in jobs we don't enjoy, in order to buy things we don't need, just to impress people we don't even like. It's insanity.

Interestingly enough, anxiety stems from focusing on ourselves too much. Think about the happiest people you know. I mean truly, lastingly happy. Are those same people also the ones constantly trying to look cool on social media or have the latest and greatest gadget? I'd imagine they are not. The happiest people I know look outside of themselves for happiness. They achieve long-term fulfillment by helping or caring for others and striving to make an impact in their communities.

We can only create such impact when we stop focusing on ourselves so intently. Focusing inward causes us to worry about our own problems and status in the world. Looking outward helps us not only appreciate what we already have, but also spread joy to others. When we pursue our own happiness first, we often find it eludes us. But when we seek impact first, the meaning and happiness we create in the world often comes back to us many times over.

I've always believed making an impact helps us achieve happiness because when we contribute to causes and missions we care about, we extend ourselves. We become a part of other people's lives and leave a mark on our communities. To our survival-based brains, this mark represents the potential for our spirit to live on long after we're physically gone from this earth. Though it's not true immortality, it's the next best thing.

FIND A MISSION YOU BELIEVE IN

A mission is a situation, assignment, or cause you find important. It could be something specific such as raising happy children, or more general, like improving race relations in the US. There is no right or wrong mission, and you can have many in your lifetime. Whatever you decide to take on as a mission, just make sure it's something you're passionate about that can make a positive difference in the lives of others.

Mission-driven work, then, is simply the work required to bring your mission closer to reality. For example, if your mission were to reduce the number of drunk-driving accidents in your town, you could give talks at your local schools to educate kids on the dangers of driving under the influence, and show them other, safe ways to have fun. Figuring out your own mission-driven work need not be that difficult, just reverse engineer what it would take to bring your mission to life, then get out there and do that work.

There are two main reasons why mission-driven work is so important when it comes to anxiety. The first is it helps us stop focusing on ourselves and our fears. Focusing on ourselves leads us to dwell on our problems. Thinking about our problems and anxiety causes them to expand. By focusing outward, we not only increase our potential for impact and fulfillment, but also lower the chance that we'll get stuck in looping-thinking over our fears.

The second reason is that mission-driven work gives us a place to channel our anxious energy when it arrives. Though working out is great, there are only so many times we can go to the gym each day. Having a mission we can work on provides us a massive outlet for channeling our apprehensions into something good.

Years ago, when I decided I would eventually write a book on living with and overcoming anxiety, I started on a new mission. That mission was to get published and help others going through the same struggles I was. That same mission is a driving force in my life today. It's what pushes me to finish writing these pages even when I'd rather watch TV, and it's the outlet I use to channel anxious energy when I'm feeling fearful.

Thinking about every person I could impact fuels me. After my writing sessions, I often feel like I'm already helping the people that will one day read this book. These are some of the most gratifying feelings I've ever felt. And I know they'll only increase once I publish and actually start helping others.

This same kind of power is available to you too. It doesn't matter if you're writing a book, building a company, or teaching children in your town. All you have to do is pick a cause or mission you believe in that will help you leave an impact. Then, figure out what work is required to get there and get moving.

WAITING FOR THE END

It was 8:00 in the morning on January 13th, 2018, on the Hawaiian island of Kauai. I still hadn't adjusted to the time zone, so I'd been getting up early to hit the gym each day, something I didn't normally do back home. On this particular morning, I'd just finished a workout and was walking back toward our villa. I opened the front door to our place and saw my dad lying on the couch in front of me. He popped up, with a puzzled look on his face.

"Did you get the alert?" he said.

"No, I didn't bring my phone with me to the gym. What alert?" I replied.

"You know, the alert. I got it on my phone and my iPad," he chimed back.

The New England Patriots were playing the Tennessee Titans in a playoff game that night. "Did Tom Brady get hurt?"

"No, it was something about a missile," Dad replied.

"A missile? Wow. That's crazy. I wonder who launched it and where it landed."

I rushed to grab my phone to see what I could find. My mind immediately jumped to the idea of the US striking North Korea or North Korea launching a warning missile in the ocean.

I opened my phone to find the alert. Nothing. I remembered I had turned off such notifications a few years prior, since most of them were flash flood warnings that didn't actually result in floods. I opened a web browser and searched *missile alert*. All of the results were tweets from the previous five minutes. People were freaking out. I kept scrolling through the results until I found a screenshot of the alert itself. I read it out loud, not truly realizing what it said until I finished:

BALLISTIC MISSILE THREAT INBOUND TO HAWAII. SEEK IMMEDIATE SHELTER. THIS IS NOT A DRILL.

"Oh my god, Dad! We're fucking dead!" My heart raced out of my chest. I felt the sudden urge to throw up. My mind plunged into the depths of darkness. I thought about how in just ten minutes or so, we'd be blown to smithereens, off the map, and gone for good. What started as a paradise vacation had quickly become a journey to hell. "Is this seriously the end? Is this how we die? At the hands of a bunch of terrorists?"

My mom, brother, sister-in-law, and nephew heard me screaming and came out into the living room. I couldn't exactly get the words out of my mouth. I didn't need to. They'd gotten the alert themselves.

My mom remained the calmest. "If this is the end, then this is the end, and there's nothing we can do about it." I knew she was right, but that didn't help me in the moment. All I felt was overwhelming anger. How could we have been so stupid to go to the closest US territory to North Korea when tensions had escalated? I couldn't believe this was our fate.

Within a minute or so, the anger turned to resounding feelings of sadness and regret. I looked at my nephew, who was not even two years old at the time. There's no way he could have known what was happening. I asked myself, "How could someone bomb a two-year-old off the face of the planet?" The thoughts were agonizing. I was drowning in a sea of my own tears.

They always say that as you sit on your deathbed, you'll regret the things you didn't do in your lifetime more than the things you did do. That morning, nothing could have been truer. I thought about how I'd been coasting along in my life for the past two years, working a job I didn't love. I thought about all the goals I'd put off for a later time.

I thought about how I let my anxiety, one way or another, make me passive at times on these big goals. Getting married, having a family, starting a company, publishing this book. All of these most important things to me, gone. My family too. Never would I get the chance to pursue these things or see these people again. I looked back at a life half-lived. It was the definition of heartbreaking.

Most of us were in shock. My parents did their best to keep our spirits high. All we could do was wait. We sat in that living room, waiting to die. It was the longest half hour of my life. Thirty-eight minutes later, my family members' phones started chiming in unison. It sounded like something out of a bad dream. Another alert. "Holy shit. This is it," I thought. "The bomb is about to drop. This is when and how we die." The tears came harder and harder.

My dad read the new message. "We're all set!"

All set?! What did that mean?

"They said the first alert was a false alarm. There is no missile threat."

The noise of the second alert kept ringing in my head for what felt like hours. Despite the fact that there was no longer a threat, I was still rattled. I couldn't stop crying. And even when the tears subsided, my anxiety didn't. Hawaii had previously seemed like a safe haven to me. A random place in the middle of the ocean. That safe haven was no longer apparent to me. Now it just seemed like a war zone. I wanted off the island.

The next day, we'd fly to California to sleep, then spend MLK day at Disneyland. But for the next thirty hours, I'd have to somehow figure out a way to get through the stress. Those thirty hours were some of the worst of my life. Minutes moved in slow motion. The Patriots game came and went. My eyes were on the television, but my mind was nowhere near it. Before I went to bed that night, I hugged all my family members and told them I loved them. I honestly thought there was a good chance we'd still get nuked that night and never see each other again.

I didn't sleep a wink. I broke into a cold sweat every time an airplane passed my window. I used a towel I'd placed next to my bed to wipe the sweat away. By the end of the night, that towel was soaked, both in perspiration and fear. The minutes continued to crawl by. I counted them down as I waited for the morning with all the lights on in my room.

Sure, the immediate threat of a strike had supposedly vanished. But we still didn't have all the answers. Had it been a complete false alarm? Had someone pushed a button by mistake, or was the alert a sign the defense department thought a strike was imminent?

After what seemed like an endless night, I got out of bed to watch another playoff football game – the Pittsburgh Steelers vs. the Jacksonville Jaguars. It certainly helped pass the time, but I still couldn't take my mind off the fact that another alert and actual missile could arrive at any moment. I wouldn't be content until we were off the island. Even the air conditioning system coming on sounded like the beginning of the end to me. As the football game neared its completion, we packed up our car and headed for the airport. The fear subsided ever so slightly.

Three hours later, after lunch at a beachside sports bar, we were on the plane, waiting for takeoff. "This is it. We might actually get out of here," I said to myself. "If we do make it home, I promise I'll take the lessons I learned on this island to heart. I'll start making changes in my life that will help me look at the next life-threatening event and say, 'I truly lived.' I'll start interviewing for new jobs, I'll finish my book and get it published within a year, and I'll ramp up my dating in hopes of finding someone with whom I could eventually start a family." As that plane zoomed down the runway, I had to fight back even more tears. We'd defied death. I'd been given a second chance and a new perspective on anxiety.

PUTTING ANXIETY IN PERSPECTIVE

The situation my family and I faced in Hawaii was by far the scariest thing I've experienced in my life. Yet while it was extremely difficult to go through at the time, I now see it as a blessing in disguise. It was a wake-up call for me, my own proverbial version of Charles Dickens' *A Christmas Carol*. It was a reminder that life is short and spending it in pursuit of anything other than your biggest passions is no life at all.

Even though I'd already developed most of the strategies in this book at the time of the missile alert, the event brought me a new perspective. It was striking to me because I felt like I was living by that perspective already. However, when that alert came, I realized I'd been fooling myself. I wasn't truly living it. I was just telling myself I was.

That new perspective was the fact that most of the things you and I get anxious about are trivial in the grand scheme of things. That's not to say they are easy to go through. It's just that while being turned down in job interviews and worrying about presentations indirectly remind our brains of our mortality, they almost never represent the true thing. Being faced with the real thing in Hawaii forced me to see this perspective and realign with it.

On the plane ride back to the continental US, that perspective spoke to me. It said, "The only thing to be afraid of in life is dying with the music still inside you. The things you typically get scared of: dates, tough conversations, and the like – those are not death. Stop worrying all the time and thinking such things are so important and just live your fucking life."

That voice was right. Even though the thought of falling apart during an interview is scary, from the perspective of death, it's a complete triviality. As long as you have life, you have everything. There are always more interviews to chase down, but you only get one life. Why waste it worrying all the time?

The challenging thing about a new perspective is it often doesn't last. When we leave the situation from which it came to us, we often go right back to our old ways of living and forget our new outlook. But this doesn't have to be the case. We can condition our new perspectives and remind ourselves of them daily.

Every night since the missile alert, before bed, I've thought back to that thirty-hour period on Kauai and said to myself, "I am really fucking lucky to be alive." Nothing actually happened on the island. No missile came. Nothing blew up. But that's not the point.

I saw the other side and was given a second chance. I don't want to get to my deathbed and have another regretful realization. I don't need another reminder. I will remind myself of that situation and my new perspective every single day. I have no more excuses. It's really time to start living. I hope you feel the same way. Because it really is time.

Waiting for the end that morning in Hawaii was an experience I'll never forget. In some ways, it made me realize we're all just waiting for the end. Life is short. We think we have forever to live when we don't. We forget about our inevitable mortality and allow things that really aren't all that important to feel like they're life or death situations, when they aren't.

When you remind yourself daily of the fact that you'll actually die one day, it can help put things in perspective for you too. During anxious situations, you can step back and say, "In the grand scheme of things, this is not that big of a deal. I will get through this. This too shall pass." Reconnecting to this kind of perspective is one of the most effective ways of developing the life of calm we've discussed in this second part of the book.

CONCLUSION: EMBRACE THE JOURNEY

When I set out to write this book, my strategy was threefold. I'd start off with a practical explanation of anxiety and describe the power of our thoughts in relation to it. With the proper foundation set, I'd introduce my framework for mitigating anxious symptoms in the middle of acute, fear-provoking situations. Finally, I'd develop various holistic approaches and habits that, when integrated into daily practice, can help cultivate a life of calm and tranquility.

Now that we've finished our exploration into all three of those topics, I hope I've left you with an invaluable set of strategies for living with your own anxiety. Tactics like slowing yourself down with methodical breathing, not resisting your anxiety, and reciting a powerful mantra are just a few of these strategies. The ones you found most helpful combine into what I would call your own personal anxiety toolkit.

Take this toolkit with you everywhere you go and leverage your favorite strategies when you're feeling especially stressed. You can't go to the gym one time and expect to be fit forever, though. You must practice these principles until they become lifelong habits. There is no magic formula that will cure your anxiety in an instant. There's only disciplined and perspective-guided thought and action. The power to put those thoughts and actions into motion is in your hands.

When I think back on the journey I've been on over the past ten or so years, I can't help but be in awe of how everything has conspired to lead me from one event to the next, to the place I am right now. It's hard for me not to think of myself as an anxious high schooler, scared to death about track meets and cute girls. It's equally as difficult to not remember the days in college where I feared running into a girl I liked and having a panic attack on the spot.

Despite the disappointment and frustration I faced at times, I think about how those hardships taught me valuable lessons, led me to bigger and better situations, and helped mold me into the person I am today. When we're in the middle of a tough situation, it's difficult to see the bigger picture at work.

We're all given our own canvas. When we move through life and start painting our masterpieces, we sometimes get caught up on the most difficult brushstrokes. Often, this myopic approach makes us lose sight of the piece of art taking shape in front of us. Though we often wish we could do without them, those tough brushstrokes serve a purpose. Without them, we might not develop the skills necessary to make our paintings even better.

I'll be completely honest with you. I still struggle with anxiety and the concepts I've described in this book from time to time. Such is life. But through many of the experiences I recounted during our time together, I've developed strategies that have helped me become more content and grounded. I shared those strategies with you so you too would have an anxiety toolkit to use in your own battles. Though there were a million reasons for writing this book, that was the main one.

At the end of the day, your mind and body are all you have. When your internal world is in peril, nothing else matters. You could get a new car or house or even win the lottery, but when you're unfathomably depressed and anxious, none of those things would truly change how you feel. In fact, most of us would probably give up all of those things just to feel better.

If there's one thing we've seen throughout our time together, it's that hell isn't just a place. It's also a mental state. If you don't take the time to cultivate a disciplined mind, you could wind up living in that fiery pit forever. Give yourself one of the most powerful gifts you can. Practice the strategies I laid out in this book daily. Cultivate a life of inner peace so you can enjoy your external circumstances alongside your tranquility.

As we close out this book, I'd like to leave you with one last thought: life really is a journey. Along the way, we often resist the twists and turns of our adventure, and that leads to much of our stress and anxiety in life. But if you knew exactly how your journey would unfold, it wouldn't be fun anymore. We need twists and turns in our lives. Uncertainty is what makes life interesting. Thank you for letting me share some of the twists and turns of my journey with you. Now get out there and embrace yours.

ACKNOWLEDGEMENTS

Many people have asked me how long it took to write this book. It's a tough question to answer. While the writing process lasted just over a year, I feel like I'd been preparing for that process since junior year of high school. So many people helped me in both the production of this work as well as the time leading up to it, and I want to use this section to thank them.

A first and massive thank you to my mother, Ann. She's always listened and supported me during my most troubling moments. In college, she brought me to all my psychiatrist appointments and paid for them herself, despite our family's high health insurance deductible. She would've done anything to help me get better. I still can't believe how selfless she was.

She was always there, at a moment's notice, to pick me up from school and take me for a ride whenever I was having a meltdown. I never realized during our conversations in mall parking lots that we were writing many of the pages of this book. I wouldn't be the man I am today without my mother, nor would I be nearly as accepting of myself. Thank you for listening, mom. I love you so much.

A special thank you to Dr. Lorraine McGee, who I consider both a spiritual teacher and a friend. She gave me invaluable advice during one of the most difficult periods of my life and later raised her hand to proofread this entire book. She sat down with me during her busy work schedule to review her comments and suggest improvements. Thank you for all your help over the years, Lorraine.

To my coach, Jason Drees, thanks for all your support and encouragement during our coaching sessions. I'll never forget your advice about the futility of pretending to be

ACKNOWLEDGEMENTS

perfect; exposing our rough edges in life is what makes us interested in and attracted to one another. Without beliefs like that one, I'm not sure I would've written this book. You helped me shoot down shame and own myself which gave me a self-confidence I so greatly needed.

Thank you to my early readers for your time and feedback. Specifically, Dan Katcher, Miguel Galvez, and Amanda Gardner. You all provided critical feedback and ideas that helped me make this book even better. I'm very grateful for your generosity.

To my editor, Angi Black, thank you for providing that outside perspective I desperately needed to shape this book into what it ultimately became. And to my illustrator, Akhil Dakinedi. Thank you for your hard work and creativity. I'm so excited with what we came up with. Angi and Akhil, both of you had a massive impact on getting this book over the finish line.

And finally, to my father, Joe, and brother, Eric. Thank you for introducing me to the worlds of spirituality, positive thinking, and personal development. Your optimism and understanding impacted the pages of this book in ways I cannot put into words.

I NEED YOUR HELP

Thank you so much for purchasing and reading *Get Out of Your Head: A Toolkit for Living with and Overcoming Anxiety*. I really hope you enjoyed it.

Before you go, I have one small favor to ask. Would you mind going to Amazon and writing a review for this book? I'm on a mission to help others with their mental health struggles, and every review I receive helps this book climb Amazon's rankings and reach new readers. With enough reviews, we can impact a large number of people.

I read all my reviews and take them very seriously. I also use them to make updates to this book and get ideas for future projects. Every little bit helps.

Thanks!

Brian

ABOUT THE AUTHOR

Brian Sachetta is a software developer, blogger, and mental health advocate. He resides in Boston, where he is happily surrounded by friends and family. If you'd like to get in touch with him, please send him an email at: brian@gooyhbook.com